THIS WORKBOOK
BELONGS TO:

The NEW RULES OF MONEY

A Playbook for Planning Your Financial Future

THE WALL STREET JOURNAL.

Bourree Lam and Julia Carpenter

Illustrations by Jess Kuronen

CLARKSON POTTER/PUBLISHERS

New York

CONTENTS

INTRODUCTION

MAYBE you bought this workbook because you thought of yourself as someone who is bad with money.

MAYBE you assumed you needed to take all your old habits and set them on fire.

MAYBE you expected to ball up your budget spreadsheet and remake your entire financial plan from scratch.

YOU MAY already be familiar with the concept of "impostor syndrome," the psychological phenomenon in which you doubt your own success and second-guess your worthiness to enter certain spaces, do particular jobs, or belong to special groups. People often discuss impostor syndrome when it comes to careers, but it can apply to our feelings about our finances, too.

WHO WE ARE

We're two people who care about helping you find ways to manage your finances. But we also know (from our own professional and personal experiences!) that talking about money can feel icky. Checking your bank app sometimes requires Herculean strength. Doing your taxes can lead to a sudden onslaught of tears, side-splitting headaches, or a procrastination jag that leads to your entire home getting cleaned.

That's why we wrote this book. We wanted to meld the stuff we know you need to know—like how to manage your debt and how to plan for money goals both big and small—with the stuff we know you already know—like how saving for a rainy day is a good idea.

Our relationship with money is one of the most important ones in our lives. And people have so many feelings about money, from good ones—the glee of payday, the pride of having paid off a loan, the feeling of "I did it!" when you make a long-saved-for purchase—to the bad ones—the guilt of having gone over budget one month or the anxiety of committing to a long-term financial plan.

The decisions we make about money reflect as much our personal aspirations as those of other people. It's not that our achievements are dictated by those who raised us, but it's just human nature to let our surroundings influence the type of things we want or the timeline we want them on. After all, who really decides what's an okay amount to spend on what? And who decides what an acceptable time frame to get out of debt is?

The answer: **it should be you.**

For the purposes of this book, we didn't want to lean too hard on complicated diagrams or overused diet metaphors. We've both flipped through our fair share of personal finance books—some highly technical, some condescendingly simplistic—and found many of the techniques lacking. We're two journalists who work at *The Wall Street Journal,* the world's most renowned and respected financial newspaper, and together we've got more than a decade of financial journalistic know-how knocking around our brains.

Bourree learned to examine how people make decisions and spend their money in her reporting for major publications like *Freakonomics, The Atlantic,* and Refinery29's Money Diaries series. She noticed how people's habits ultimately make all the difference. Turns out, having more money isn't always the key to unlocking a personal finance genius level. Sometimes it's the person with the high paycheck who has the worst money habits.

Julia writes about the finances of different generations, in particular researching how the current financial systems and expectations are impacting the futures of today's young adults. People of all ages and backgrounds won't share the same money concerns, decisions, or dreams. In her many years reporting, she found that oftentimes, what was realistic for one generation simply isn't possible for another.

A "nest egg" is the money you save and grow for your future self. You'll see the nest egg character pop up throughout this book. As you work your way through the exercises, watch this nest egg get bigger, stronger, and more confident.

WHY DO WE NEED NEW RULES OF MONEY?

This book isn't meant to be a one-size-fits-all bible to address everything in your financial life.

So don't think of it as a textbook or a guidebook as much as a workbook. We want you to have a pen handy so that as you work through the pages **you can figure out your own answers.**

We combined over a decade of financial reporting experience with our knowledge of decision-making, habit-forming, and common sense to create a book that won't just offer Band-Aids to your current problems but instead will help you plan a way forward for short-term and long-term goals.

Each section comes complete with the following:

- A detailed and researched explanation of an important money concept to master.

- Some tools that help you take that concept into the real world.

- Then (and most importantly, in our opinion), a challenge or activity that can help you apply all this knowledge directly to your individual life.

As we designed the major sections of this book, we took inspiration from some other works we admired. And no, we weren't reviewing personal finance books, economic textbooks, or even history books. We looked somewhere a little unexpected: to cookbooks.

Both of us love cooking. We especially love how anyone, regardless of cooking skills, can flip through a cookbook and get something out of it, either by returning to a simple classic (the perfect poached egg, for Bourree, who likes to master the small stuff) or challenging yourself with something a little more involved (like Julia's commitment to making one hundred bakes in 2020).

Many books in the personal finance genre tend to be confessional or dictionary-like. And while there's a lot of value to be gained from reading more about another person's experience and money decisions, just as there's a lot of value in learning about financial products and concepts, neither of these types of books is totally clear on how to personalize that knowledge **for your own life.**

This personal finance "cookbook" will show you step-by-step how to achieve the financial goals that are important to you. It's both "choose your own adventure" and "rinse and repeat"; it's also about automating these routines so they easily fit into your busy life.

Why do recipes work for personal finance? Recipes are instructional and tried and true. The format is straightforward and gives you a more guaranteed result than if you were to wing it. Importantly, it takes the emotions out of the equation. A recipe has also been tested, so you don't have to worry about going through all the trial and error. (Because who has time for that?)

This "cookbook" also allows for personalization. It's useful to both beginners and those with more experience, as we've heard from the thousands of *Wall Street Journal* readers who have done our personal finance "recipes." For example, if you're saving for retirement and want to just use a 401(k) account from your company, that's what works for you. Others may choose to have additional accounts for more flexibility, but you may not need that.

Lastly, the reason customizing personal finance know-how is so important is that not everyone is starting at the same point on the road. Some of you reading this will be coming from backgrounds where money was scarce and knowledge hoarded; others of you may have grown up with significant financial resources already at your fingertips. Some may be debt-free while others cringe every time they check their credit card statement. One person may look to this workbook for help in one specific area of personal finance, while others may open it not knowing quite where to begin.

The exercises in this book build on one another, with the idea that we will show you how different mechanisms of your financial health— goal-setting, saving, debt management, investing, and more—have to work together.

We know this stuff is stressful! We're not pretending it's not! But we're telling you: it's possible.

A FINE-PRINT NOTE:
We are journalists, not financial
advisers or fiduciaries. If you are seeking
professional advice, please consult
a financial planner. Our suggestions are
limited to the types of products investors may
want to consider as part of their financial
planning, and are based on our reporting.
We don't have affiliations or ties with
financial companies and are not
compensated for our views.

LET'S GET STARTED

01 01

Okay. Take a deep breath. Roll your shoulders. Brew some tea. Put on the calmest playlist you can find, like "spa sounds" or "ocean noises" or something. Pet your dog, or your cat, or the fuzziest pillow in your apartment.

This should be the easiest, least stressful page of the whole book! And hey, take solace in this: opening this personal finance book isn't going to be as scary as reading about money may have felt in the past.

> **Tip:** A financial plan is all about being intentional and not letting money simply pass through your account from one month to the next. In this workbook, we're not just buying groceries; we're making a meal plan.

First, let's set your intentions. Why did you choose this book?

_____

_____

_____

_____

_____

_____

_____

What are your earliest memories about finances? Who taught you about money (the good lessons and the bad!)? How might they have influenced how you view your own finances?

MEMORY 1:

_____

_____

MEMORY 2:

_____

_____

MEMORY 3:

_____

_____

MEMORY 4:

_____

_____

MEMORY 5:

_____

_____

WHAT KIND OF MONEY PERSON ARE YOU?

- I am good / not good with money.

- I know / don't know enough about money.

- I feel good / do not feel good about spending money.

- I think I need to save more / save less.

- I think I'm financially prepared / not financially prepared for the next five years.

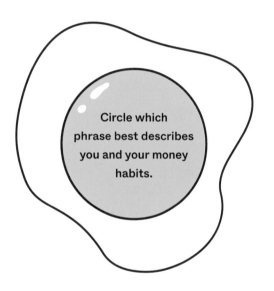

Circle which phrase best describes you and your money habits.

What do you want to change or learn about your relationship with money?

_____

_____

_____

_____

LET'S GET COOKING

WHAT FINANCIAL INGREDIENTS DO YOU WANT TO LEARN MORE ABOUT?

What's in your "financial pantry" already? What do other people you know have in their financial pantry that you think you might need?

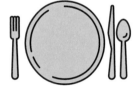

LIST THEM BELOW:

HOW TO USE THIS BOOK

The point at which your financial life starts doesn't have to be a specific age or a specific life event. In fact, it's mostly up to you where to draw the starting line.

For some, it was when they first got an allowance or took out a loan. Others point to the moment they finally became in charge of their own money and began mapping out their various expenses.

There are still other moments that people we've talked to say was the start of their financial life: it's when they graduated from college and got a paycheck and debt payments to take care of; it's when they first purchased a car or home and had to learn about interest rates and down payments; some wouldn't consider their financial lives started until they had children and finally started planning for the long term.

> **Tip:** You may begin this book as an individual, but you also may be someone who shares money and financial goals with a partner. Ask for their input and insight as you work your way through the exercises. Don't assume your goals are their goals.

WHAT DO I NEED TO START MY FINANCIAL LIFE?

Think about it as making soup. You begin with broth, then maybe you add some vegetables, herbs, and beans, and maybe some meat if you'd like. As you let the soup stew over time, it gets more layered in flavor.

A financial life is similar in that you build up the tools to manage your money slowly, and your finances get more complex over time. How complex you want to make them is up to you, since there are many tools for you to choose from that can automate and do the work for you—just like when you're adding more spices and herbs to your soup or electing to keep it simple and brothy.

Here's the important thing: get prepared for whichever stage you're at—the other stuff can come later. You don't need to digest an avalanche of information about the financial tools you don't yet need. Instead, build the toolkit you need for your financial life now, and you'll get to the rest when you reach your next stage.

This chapter will go over the basic ingredients every person needs. We will also go over how to pick the right financial products and financial documents for the different stages of life. If you already know the basics, feel free to skim this chapter, or read it carefully to refresh your memory and boost your confidence. And hey, we may have a few things in there that may be relevant for you still.

BUILD THE TOOLKIT YOU NEED

FOR YOUR FINANCIAL LIFE NOW.

FIND YOUR STARTING LINE

Some people feel their starting line is determined by someone—or something—else. "My starting line is graduating from school." "I'll know my starting line whenever I dig out of this debt."

We want you to think of this journey a little differently. Consider it this way: if someone else is setting the starting line, then someone else is setting the endpoint, too. This book is designed to help you take control of that process and set those markers in a way that makes the most sense for you.

No matter what your starting line is, it's important to be there for yourself. Take advantage of the energy that comes with starting a new chapter in your life—the boost can do a lot for your personal motivation.

In our experience, all of these "moments" are valid as the start of one's financial life. Every time you reach one of these milestones, there are things you'll need to feel equipped for what's in store. The key is not to look back with regret. The point is to start now and don't hesitate. You don't want to get stuck by letting all the things you think you should know about money stop you from taking action.

Let's find your starting line.

None of us start in the same place. Maybe you have a lot of student debt. (Or none!) Maybe you're someone who didn't pay your own bills until after college or your first job. Maybe you're someone who has been financially independent since sixteen. Or maybe you never thought about finances until you had to combine your life with someone else. Don't compare; you're on your own journey.

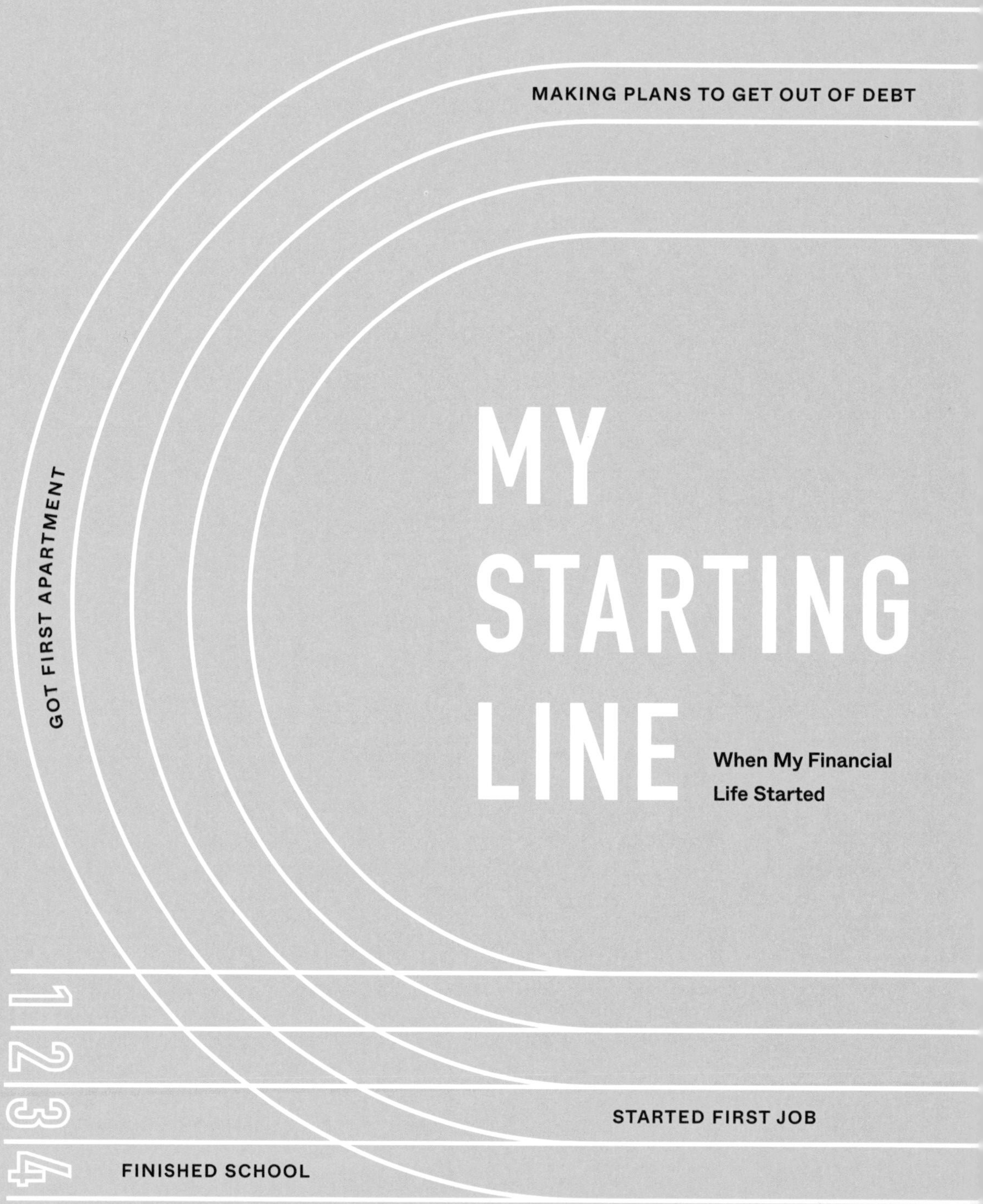

MAKING PLANS TO GET OUT OF DEBT

GOT FIRST APARTMENT

MY
STARTING
LINE

**When My Financial
Life Started**

1
2
3
4

STARTED FIRST JOB

FINISHED SCHOOL

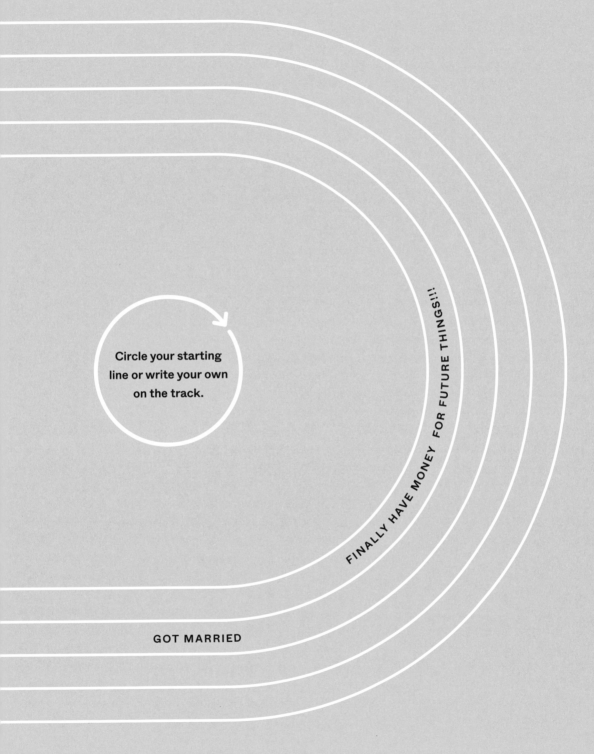

Circle your starting line or write your own on the track.

FINALLY HAVE MONEY FOR FUTURE THINGS!!!

GOT MARRIED

WHEN YOU'RE READY
FOR THE BASICS

Open a Personal Checking and Savings Account

A checking account allows you to deposit and withdraw money via an ATM, checkbook, or banking app. You'll also find it useful for paying off bills and credit cards. To pick the right one, find a bank where you meet the minimum threshold to avoid fees. Minimize fees by confirming it's free to use their ATMs or debit cards, and that there are ATMs at convenient locations where you live and go out. If you transfer money often, it'll be helpful for your bank to have services such as Zelle.

Track Your Expenses

Whether you use an Excel sheet or a physical journal as a money diary, keeping track of your expenses is a good habit to get into right away. Recording every purchase may seem stressful at first, but it will allow you to see how your money is going in and coming out of your various accounts. Tracking your expenses also helps you find what areas you may want to focus on as you start to add financial goals to your life. Some banks have simple breakdown categories of the areas your transactions are in. That's good, but for a more detailed approach use software such as Mint or YNAB (You Need a Budget). An old-school spreadsheet is also an excellent offline way to track your expenses.

Apply for One Credit Card, with Either Cash Back or Rewards You'll Use

By now you've probably received at least one or two mailings saying you've been approved for a credit card. Pick wisely, as you'll want to stick to using at least one card regularly to build your credit history over several years (more on this concept in later chapters). We have a friend who still uses her first card for her Spotify subscription, and another built his credit history by using his card for groceries. For right now, the easiest way to ensure you're taking advantage of perks is to pick a cash-back card. The most competitive offers will have no annual fee and offer up to 5% cash back on your purchases as well as some kind of introductory offer. Also remember: automate your minimum payments while you're setting up your account so you never get hit with penalty fees. Always pay off your full balance every month.

Nail Down Your Debt Repayment Schedule

If you took out student loans for your education, start paying attention to the balance as soon as you graduate. Repayment starts as soon as you leave school or drop down to taking classes part-time.

For certain types of federal student loans, there are grace periods, during which you don't have to repay your loans yet. For Direct Subsidized, Direct Unsubsidized, or Federal Family Education Loans, the grace period is six months. It's an initial nine months for Perkins Loans.

Take advantage of the grace period. This is a great time to figure out whether you want to do the Standard Repayment Plan or another repayment plan.

WHEN YOU'VE JUST STARTED YOUR FIRST JOB

Fill Out W-4 and 1040 Forms

Welcome to the wonderful world of taxes. You've arrived. Having your first job means a paycheck but also filing federal and state taxes. Your employer will probably ask you to fill out a W-4 form as part of your onboarding, which will allow them to withhold income taxes from your paycheck, which is a) required by the law and b) ideal because you won't be stuck with a huge amount to pay come Tax Day (which is typically April 15, so mark it on your calendar now).

Then every April, it's time to file your taxes to see if you get a tax refund, money that was withheld during the year that you get back because you overpaid. Here's where you figure out if you're able to claim various deductions and tax breaks, which will lower the amount you owe. Most people with simple tax situations will use Form 1040 and take the Standard Deduction.

Tip: Anyone can file a federal tax return free through the Free File program on the Internal Revenue Service's site (www.irs.gov/freefile). Those under an income threshold can use the Guided Tax Preparation option.

Void a Check

Your employer may also ask you for a voided check in order to process direct deposit of your paycheck. You can get this from your bank by requesting a checkbook. Then take a marker and write VOID across the front of the check, and attach it to your signed direct deposit form. Direct deposit is the fastest way to access your pay on payday, and you can keep a copy of the check (saved safely!) for future reference in case you're wondering what happened to it.

Start Your 401(k) or Individual Retirement Account

Don't skimp on your retirement account! When you create a 401(k), you're agreeing to move a certain percentage of your income into this account so it will grow over time. Many employers offer a match if you meet a certain contribution threshold. That means as a benefit, they will tack on an extra percentage to your contribution, sometimes 1% or 2% and sometimes even higher. That is free money deposited into your retirement account, so pay attention during your human resources overview and initial job onboarding. If the employer offers an employee match, set your contribution amount to the level that would maximize the match, if you can afford it. Don't worry about this being set in stone: you can always change your contribution amount if you need more cash. But in the meantime, automating retirement savings in a 401(k) or IRA is one of the smartest things you can do to grow your money over the years.

WHEN YOU'RE READY
TO RENT AN APARTMENT

Buy a Cashier's Check

Some landlords don't take personal checks or cash. In those instances, you'll want to buy a cashier's check from your bank to give them the deposit. Typically, a deposit is one to three months of the monthly rent amount, so make sure you've saved before starting the process.

You can visit your bank and ask a teller for a cashier's check, and some institutions allow you to order cashier's checks online. Important: treat this piece of paper as literal money; if you lose it, that money is gone.

Get Renter's Insurance

People often neglect to insure things in their apartment, but renters should get a yearly policy to protect against theft or other types of loss. Rental insurance is much easier to buy than other types of insurance and can be finalized online. Find a policy with an acceptable deductible, such as $500 or $1,000, so you are insured for losses above that amount.

Are you sick of renting an apartment? Flip to page 126.

WHEN YOU HAVE SOME EXTRA MONEY

Open a High-Yield Savings Account for Emergency Savings

You should have at least three months of monthly expenses saved in an emergency savings account. That includes rent, food, expenses, and any monthly debt payments. Once you've built your emergency savings, then you can consider investing.

Your rainy-day fund should be easily accessible so you won't have to wait long to get your hands on the funds. Also, you'll want it to earn as much interest for you as possible so that the amount you're saving grows over time. Look for a high-yield savings account, which will pay you more interest on your cash than your typical, run-of-the-mill savings account. If you're sure you don't need the money for a year or two, you can look into certificates of deposit (CDs). Some CDs offer flexibility and no penalty for early withdrawals.

Start an Investment Account

If you're all set on your emergency savings, consider opening a brokerage account or investment account to start growing your cash in the stock market. This is only a good option if you're willing to be a long-term investor (more on that in Chapter 8). The key to picking a good brokerage account is to make sure your trades are free and that buying fractional shares is an option.

IF YOU DECIDE
TO HAVE A KID

Open a 529 Account

Congratulations! You're going to be a parent!

In addition to the changing table, toy chest, and other baby-rearing necessities, you're also going to need a plan to pay for your child's education. A 529 account is a special savings plan used for college tuition and other educational expenses. Anyone can open a 529—a godparent, grandmother, or family friend—and stashing money there allows your money to grow. The money grows tax-free and you can make tax-free withdrawals for educational expenses.

> **Tip:** If you are parenting with a spouse or a partner, don't forget to establish an open line of communication with them as you set up this account. This will create a strong foundation for your joint parenting journey. Let the grandparents know, too.

WHEN YOU PICK HEALTH INSURANCE ACCOUNTS

Find Health Insurance

When you get your first job, you might still be on your parents' health insurance. But by the time you turn twenty-six, you need to have your own health insurance, either a plan provided through your employer or, if you're self-employed, a plan you buy or find through the Affordable Care Act (the Marketplace). You'll want to pay extra attention during open enrollment every year to reassess what kind of plan works for you.

Start a Flexible Spending Account, or FSA

Some employer-sponsored health-care plans come with specific savings accounts for health-care expenses. Your employer deducts a certain amount from your pay before tax to put into this bucket, which you then use for your health-care expenses in a given year.

Invest in a Health Savings Account, or HSA

If you have a high-deductible plan, you can have a Health Savings Account, another type of account that comes with major tax benefits. But the individual is in charge of the HSA, not the employer, and any amount you don't use will roll over into the following year.

WHAT I NEED IN MY LIFE

WHAT FINANCIAL INGREDIENTS DO YOU WANT TO LEARN MORE ABOUT?

Write down financial ingredients from the previous pages you need to add to your financial "soup":

1. _____
2. _____
3. _____
4. _____
5. _____
6. _____
7. _____
8. _____
9. _____
10. _____

Take advantage of the energy that comes with starting a new chapter in your life—the boost can do a lot for your personal motivation.

MAKE YOUR OWN
02 MILESTONES 02

Living free of other people's expectations is hard, but even harder to handle are the money expectations you have for yourself.

You spot a friend or acquaintance on social media posing with a pair of shiny keys and standing beside a **SOLD** sign. Chatting with friends at happy hour reveals that more of them have paid off their student loans than you thought. One day you look up and it feels like everyone else has moved on from roommate life, but you can't find a way to live on your own and still pay your bills.

But having expectations is a normal part of being a human who lives among other humans. We've all had the "Am I . . . doing it wrong?" panic in the middle of the night (if you haven't, it's only a matter of time). This is especially true when it comes to money. You might find yourself thinking, How much money should I be making? Spending? Saving? What's normal for someone like me?

DON'T FEEL
THE PRESSURE

Our ideas of timelines and big milestones are set for us by our parents, our culture, our peer groups, and, of course, ourselves. Sifting through those various ideas to define what "success" means for you can feel all-consuming, to say the least. Let's clarify the differences.

List other people's expectations for themselves:

_____

_____

_____

_____

_____

_____

_____

_____

_____

_____

_____

_____

List other people's expectations for you:

_____

_____

_____

_____

_____

_____

_____

_____

_____

_____

_____

_____

_____

_____

_____

_____

_____

_____

_____

_____

Now cross out the ones that aren't you, don't fit your money personality, or somehow can't connect to the words you wrote down earlier in this book.

DECIDE WHAT
YOU WANT

What are your expectations for yourself?

Which of those feel doable?

Which feel impossible?

YOU *DECIDE* WHAT FINANCIAL

MILESTONES ARE RIGHT FOR YOU.

We like to think of shedding preconceived ideas as peeling back the layers in a garlic clove. Once upon a time, we dreaded seeing "garlic" in an ingredients list. Peeling cloves is a messy job, and the skins would shred off in tiny scraps and get under our fingernails. (Not to mention the smell.) We would feel frustrated by the process, or sometimes even feel tempted to skip the garlic altogether.

But then a dear friend showed us a trick to peeling garlic cloves: you pour boiling water over the clove and the skins peel off so much more easily. Now we do this meal prep—a kitchen chore we once dreaded!—with ease.

Getting the hang of shedding expectations can be like that, too. Learn something new, then just do it once, and soon enough you'll find yourself doing it all the time. Here's how to map out your timeline and goals and decide what makes sense for your money.

> **Tip:** Start small. If it's too overwhelming to set financial goals for your entire life, start by structuring your spending and saving plan on a much smaller scale. Noticing the little things week to week is so important. Be sure to also notice your tiny wins along the way!

PICK YOUR BATTLES

Setting goals can feel overwhelming, underwhelming, or somewhere in between.

Some people find themselves flooded with to-dos—"pay down my debt," "buy a house," and more—and others struggle to see beyond the immediate concerns—"get that promotion." Aspiring to all these things is good! But getting crushed by how overwhelming they seem, or wanting to achieve all of them at the same time, will set you back.

We have an activity that can help you see goals as realistic, attainable, and yes, even motivating. The tricky thing: you can't do too much, but the things you do have to work together. You'll likely find goal-setting works best for you when said goals work in concert with each other.

Working with one goal may help you realize new things about another; for example, writing down "I want to be debt-free" as one of your goals doesn't mean anything until you record the exact amount of debt you're working to pay off. Maybe recording your numbers will change the urgency you feel around a goal, once you see the reality of what you're working toward.

That is the point of the next exercise: prioritizing. You can't go on your dream vacation and buy a home in five years and launch your own business and go to every wedding. But you can do some of these things, and learning to understand what's achievable in what time frame is one of the most difficult things to do in personal finance.

YOUR TOP FIVE FINANCIAL GOALS

Defining realistic, specific goals is important. Too often, new-goal enthusiasts set themselves up for failure with lofty targets or vague ideas. It's the difference between "I want to exercise more" and "I will sign up for a weekly yoga class with my two other friends who also want to exercise more." Let's set realistic goals for you now.

Step 1

Out of the word cloud below, circle at least 3 or 4 financial goals and add 1 or 2 of your own so that you have 5 financial goals.

Own a home
Take a break from work
Pay off my student loans
Take a once-in-a-lifetime vacation
Pay down a credit card

Break an expensive habit
Open an investing account
Reach $_____ in savings
Start my own business
Increase my retirement contributions

More Goals:

Step 2

Now prioritize your 5 goals, from most important to you to least important. Pay attention to the "to you" part—don't just put the one you think your parents think is "best" up at the top! Think about what milestone will mean the most to you if (and when) you achieve it. We'll return to this list in future chapters.

1. _____
2. _____
3. _____
4. _____
5. _____

Add a star to the goal listed that you'll accomplish this year.

Goal-setting works best when your goals work in concert with each other.

Step 3

Next, we'll make a timeline for the goal you starred in Step 2. Write down three mini-steps you can take to accomplish it (like the example below) and assign check-in dates.

Example:

* My goal is to take a once-in-a-lifetime vacation.

* First, I'm going to price out every step of the trip, from flight prices to hotels to estimates for dining out, activities, and other extraneous costs.

* Then, I'm going to open a separate savings account to collect the money I need for this trip.

* After that, I'm going to set up (manageably sized!) automatic deposits to my savings account.

THIS IS THE GOAL I WILL ACCOMPLISH THIS YEAR

Three mini-steps I will take to achieve this goal:

1. _____

2. _____

3. _____

My check-in dates:

____ / ____ / _____   ____ / ____ / _____

____ / ____ / _____   ____ / ____ / _____

____ / ____ / _____   ____ / ____ / _____

____ / ____ / _____   ____ / ____ / _____

YOUR ★ GOAL

Step 4

Now think of someone who will help you along the way and write down their name below. Maybe it's your best friend, of whom you can ask questions—"How did you and your partner buy that first house anyway?"—or maybe it's a financial planner who can give you info—"I want to start investing but I don't know how!"—or maybe it's someone else who will champion your goal.

Who will keep you accountable for your ★ goal?

_____

_____

_____

_____

_____

_____

_____

_____

_____

THINGS WE SHOULDN'T WORRY ABOUT

Listen, you can't plan for everything. And just like you can't plan for everything, you can't worry about everything. Write down some worries you might have.

Our Worry List

Living without roommates

Paying off student loans

Buying a car

Figuring out life insurance

Making savings goal this month

Doing our taxes by ourselves (this is why we have accountants!)

Buying a house

Handling an unexpected medical bill

Saving enough for retirement

Coping with a layoff

Financially supporting a family member or loved one

Your Worry List

_____

_____

_____

_____

_____

_____

_____

_____

_____

_____

_____

_____

_____

_____

_____

_____

_____

_____

Now put a big X through the entire list to tell your mind that you're not going to worry about these things for the time being.

Don't let your worries hold you back.

BE SMART

The goals you set should be SMART. You may have come across this acronym before, and it's used by many financial planners and even the Consumer Financial Protection Bureau's education guides. There's a good reason why so many folks rely on it. Research shows that writing down SMART[1] goals help people achieve those same aims. This is what it means:

* **S**pecific

* **M**easurable

* **A**chievable

* **R**elevant

* **T**ime bound

This framework is used to set goals that feel doable. Take your goal from page 53 and write down the ways your goal is SMART.

_____

_____

_____

1. George T. Doran first coined SMART in a 1981 issue of *Management Review.*

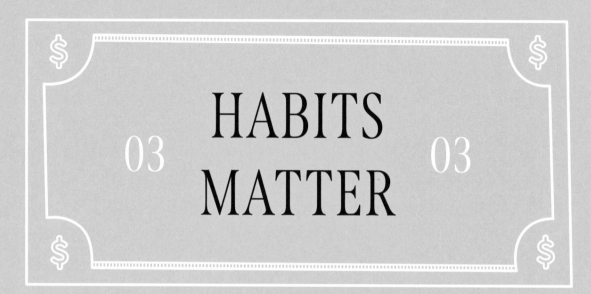

HABITS MATTER

03

03

We're about to tell you one of the biggest secrets of personal finance. It's not about buying some unknown thing that will triple your money overnight. It's not about a penny-pinching hack we know you'll love.

It's about habits, and they matter a lot.

Often when we ask people where they learned their financial habits, the answer we get is personal: from their mom, a savvy relative, a roommate who was great at cost sharing, an acquaintance who works in finance, or something they read somewhere ("but I can't remember where"). Money habits can be learned, but they can also be inherited from experience and the people in our lives.

Financial habits are important because they help us put ourselves on autopilot during times of stress, whether it's markets falling or holiday shopping. If you have good habits, you don't have to react adversely in the moment.

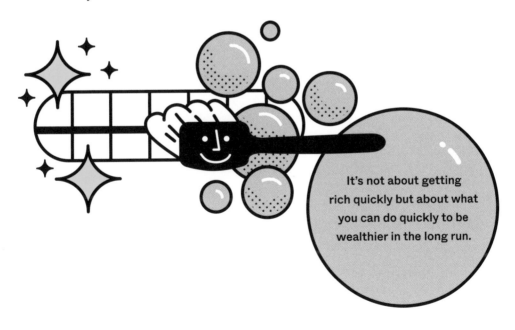

It's not about getting rich quickly but about what you can do quickly to be wealthier in the long run.

START SMALL

Little changes matter. Circle the little changes below that you would like to adopt. These are all things you should be able to do quickly and (relatively) painlessly.

- Set up an automated $10 deduction from your checking account that goes into a savings account.

- Cut a subscription, any subscription!

- Do a no-spend day once a month.

- Look at your account balance once a week.

- Balance your checking account every two weeks.

- When you find a nonessential item you want to buy, leave it in your cart for forty-eight hours (or if you're shopping in person, put it down and come back in two days) to see if you still want it.

- Find an hour a month to learn about your own finances and research questions you may have.

- Have a money conversation with someone in your life.

The great thing about money habits is that they're easy and you've likely already done them before at some point. Think of the times you've tricked yourself into not shopping or pretended money wasn't there so you couldn't spend it. Putting change in a jar is a money ritual, too, and so is picking up a bottle of wine or a candy bar every payday.

If you're still not convinced, know that habits also correlate with better financial well-being, according to research by the Consumer Financial Protection Bureau (CFPB). Those who save regularly, as a habit, report having higher levels of financial well-being and financial control compared to those who save whatever is left over at the end of the month.

Ask yourself: When did you last set a new habit and stick to it? What worked? What didn't?

THOSE
WHO SAVE
REGULARLY,
AS A HABIT,
REPORT

HAVING HIGHER LEVELS OF FINANCIAL WELL-BEING.

KEEP THE GOOD ONES, DITCH THE BAD ONES

Getting rid of financial habits or rituals that are no longer relevant to your life is hard. Whether you learned it from family or a favorite author, it's not easy to let go of something that was once useful, to acknowledge that you've moved on.

But doing so will help you financially, and reassessing and restrategizing at different points in your life is crucial.

We've seen this at work in our own lives: we've both set hard limits for the amount we'll pay for something. For Julia, it's shampoo (no more than $8). For Bourree, it's birthdays ($100 max, for anyone including herself). We've both held hard to these numbers for years, believing that because these habits got us through tough times before, they will continue to help us.

This is why habits are so hard to shake: they're built on memories and trust. Admitting that a habit, one you've prided yourself on having, no longer works for your life is tough. When inflation started to raise prices for all Americans, we both had to become flexible about these long-held beliefs.

It takes lots of mental strength and energy to maintain our financial lives, but it can be so much easier if you make your finances a matter of habits.

YOUR EVERYDAY HABITS

In the two columns below, write down all the good life habits you already have (they don't have to be financially related). Maybe you floss every single night or never forget to water your plants. In the other, write down all the less-than-good life habits you have, the ones you want to lose.

GOOD LIFE HABITS

BAD LIFE HABITS

Where did you learn those habits? Pick one from each column and elaborate more using the lines below.

LIFE HABIT (GOOD OR BAD)   **WHERE YOU LEARNED IT**

1. _____   _____

2. _____   _____

3. _____   _____

4. _____   _____

5. _____   _____

6. _____   _____

7. _____   _____

8. _____   _____

9. _____   _____

10. _____   _____

LET'S DO AN EXORCISM ON YOUR BAD MONEY HABITS

Step 1

Now let's look at your financial habits. In the columns below, write down five habits you have when it comes to saving and spending money. Include both good and bad habits, with a focus of getting those bad habits onto the page so we can rid your life of them.

Think about the origins of these habits. Identify whether they came from a parent, a friend, a money blog post from the year 2000, or a book you read. Writing all this down will help you be more objective about your financial strategies—and **identify if you've adopted these habits without analyzing whether they serve your financial goals.**

FINANCIAL HABIT   **WHERE YOU LEARNED IT**

1. _____   _____

2. _____   _____

3. _____   _____

4. _____   _____

5. _____   _____

Step 2

Once you've identified your financial habits, write down your top five financial goals from Chapter 2. If you couldn't settle on five concrete goals, write down your top three.

Goal #1: _____

_____

_____

Goal #2: _____

_____

_____

Goal #3: _____

_____

_____

Goal #4: _____

_____

_____

Goal #5: _____

_____

_____

Step 3

Let's combine the findings of Step 1 and Step 2 by looking at your goals and financial habits together so we can see if they make sense. Are the habits you developed helping you accomplish your goals in the time frame you hope? Or are the habits counterproductive?

Use the space below to match the goal with the habit that might be related—whether it's a habit that's supposed to help you reach the goal or one that might be standing in your way. Here's what that can look like:

FINANCIAL GOAL		HELPFUL OR UNHELPFUL HABIT
Saving for a down payment	→	*Automating savings monthly*
Increasing my 401K contribution	→	*Keeping track of spending*
Getting a new dress for my friend's wedding	→	*Buying the first thing you like without comparison shopping*

Match up your goals and good or bad habits here:

FINANCIAL GOAL   **HELPFUL OR UNHELPFUL HABIT**

1. _____   _____

2. _____   _____

3. _____   _____

4. _____   _____

5. _____   _____

Step 4

Consider these combinations of goals and habits with the following in mind. Which ones are:

1. Working well, and don't need tweaking.

2. Could be better, so let's make some tweaks.

3. Just aren't working or relevant anymore, so let's do away with them.

Step 5

Revisit the goals and habits that fell into the second category (the ones that could be better with some tweaks) and make the tweaks you need in the space below. At the end of this activity, you should come away with a few realistic goals and specific habits that are contributing to you achieving them.

Rewrite your realistic goals and specific habits that will help you achieve them:

FINANCIAL GOAL	SUPPORTING HABIT
1.	
2.	
3.	
4.	
5.	

HOW TO YOLO RESPONSIBLY

One core concept of personal finance is the impact short-term decisions have on long-term plans. As humans, we often struggle to make long-term decisions, while immediate ones feel easy because we have all the information we need to live for today.

That's why YOLO (you only live once) feels so good. But what happens after you YOLO is something you should learn about yourself. Do your short-term or impulse decisions lead to lasting satisfaction? What are your patterns around the things that make you happy immediately, and do those things make you happy a year later?

Let's do an activity to find out. Think of a YOLO purchase you made within the past year. Maybe it was a new bike you bought, a trip you spontaneously booked, or a massage you treated yourself to. Think about how the purchase felt in the moment. Then reflect on how you felt about the purchase six months later. Fill out the meters with your satisfaction levels.

There's no shame in living in the moment, but the goal of this activity is to find some patterns and identify your good YOLO impulses. Those good YOLO purchases are the things that you feel pretty good about weeks or months after you bought them.

First, think of a YOLO purchase you made. Write down what date you bought it, what you were doing at the time, and whether you made the purchase in person or on your device.

Now, shade in the meter with how satisfied you were with the purchase at the time.

Then, shade in the next meter to indicate how satisfied you were with the purchase six months later. Or if it hasn't been six months yet, how you feel about it now.

Do the two match up roughly? If so, this is likely a good YOLO purchase because it gave you that jolt of satisfaction up front and lasting satisfaction.

If the two don't match up, then you'll want to note these types of purchases for when they come up again in the future. Know that this type of purchase isn't likely to bring you lasting satisfaction, and whether you still think it's worth it. (The answer may be yes! But now you know.)

MY YOLO PURCHASE:

YOLO SATISFACTION THEN:

YOLO SATISFACTION NOW:

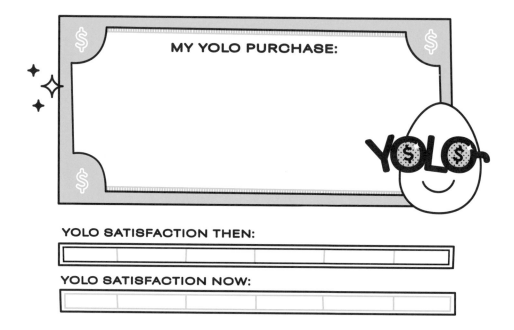

MY YOLO PURCHASE:

YOLO SATISFACTION THEN:

YOLO SATISFACTION NOW:

MY YOLO PURCHASE:

YOLO SATISFACTION THEN:

YOLO SATISFACTION NOW:

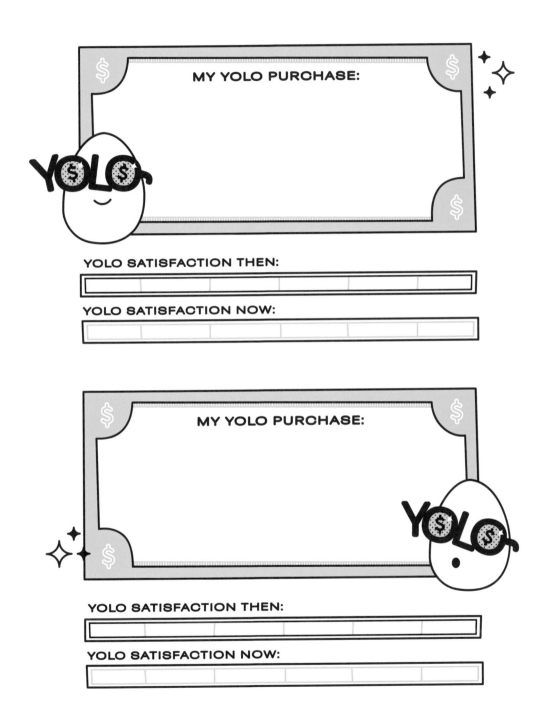

MY YOLO PURCHASE:

YOLO SATISFACTION THEN:

YOLO SATISFACTION NOW:

MY YOLO PURCHASE:

YOLO SATISFACTION THEN:

YOLO SATISFACTION NOW:

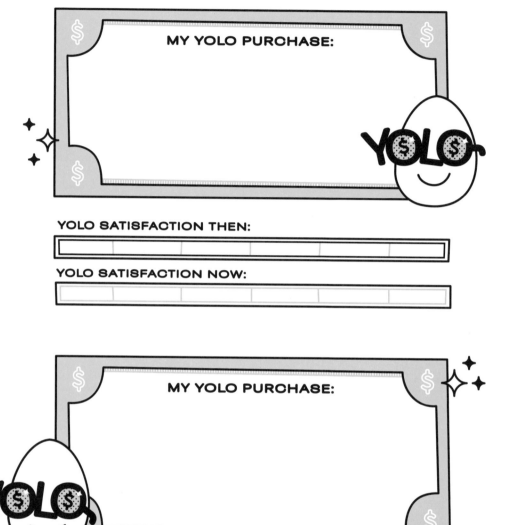

MY YOLO PURCHASE:

YOLO SATISFACTION THEN:

YOLO SATISFACTION NOW:

MY YOLO PURCHASE:

YOLO SATISFACTION THEN:

YOLO SATISFACTION NOW:

MY YOLO PURCHASE:

YOLO SATISFACTION THEN:

YOLO SATISFACTION NOW:

MY YOLO PURCHASE:

YOLO SATISFACTION THEN:

YOLO SATISFACTION NOW:

MY YOLO PATTERNS

What reoccurrences did you notice when reviewing the previous
activity? Star the realization that surprised you the most.
Take a look at the patterns you identified.

Write down three lessons you can take away from them:

Lesson 1: _____

_____

_____

_____

Lesson 2: _____

_____

_____

_____

Lesson 3: _____

_____

_____

_____

GUIDING YOUR
IMPULSE ASPIRATIONS

Impulse buying initially feels good because you're acting on a whim and scoring the sweet, sweet hit of instant gratification. But taking a moment to breathe or sit quietly can allow that whim to pass.

What are some things you think you want because you've seen photos of them on social media or elsewhere?

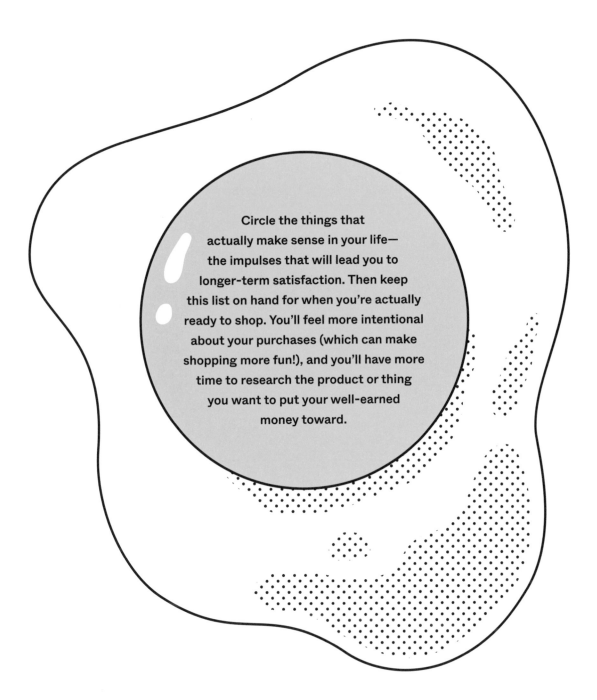

Circle the things that actually make sense in your life—the impulses that will lead you to longer-term satisfaction. Then keep this list on hand for when you're actually ready to shop. You'll feel more intentional about your purchases (which can make shopping more fun!), and you'll have more time to research the product or thing you want to put your well-earned money toward.

KNOW YOUR NUMBERS

04

You may have this ambient sense that you're not doing great. One scroll through Instagram and it seems everyone else is sitting down to extravagant brunches, taking lavish vacations, or flashing the keys of their new house or car.

You don't feel like them, though. You say things all the time like "I'm broke—AGAIN" or "Where did all my money go?" or "I don't know how to money."

There's another side to this, too. Maybe over the last handful of years, you've saved a fair chunk of change. Maybe you're thinking, My money can do it all . . . and if not, my credit card's got it.

Some of us have weathered our fair share of financial booms and busts, and many of us millennials are still bearing scars from the 2008 recession and the financial catastrophes brought on by the pandemic. Others have bought into YOLO philosophy since nothing long term feels possible; and others are living life one pay period to the next.

But here's the thing: until you actually know your numbers—and write them out, in order and in context—you can't tell which of these feelings is founded in reality and which is founded in fear or delusion. So maybe you're telling yourself your finances are not okay, or they're better than okay, but . . . do you actually know that?

Too often we think of our finances more emotionally than tangibly. We open our bank accounts and we see a number, and we don't recognize its real-world meaning; we instead think "that's good" or "that's bad."

This actually makes a lot of sense! Money is an emotional thing and, depending on your particular situation, those emotions may never evaporate entirely. We all approach money differently, and our individual backgrounds and life experiences shape how we see our own financial futures.

Before you begin, how do you feel about your numbers in general? Do you feel you know them? Or do you want more clarity? What other emotions do you hold around money and why? If you're stuck on where to start, consider the following: "When I look at my bank account, I feel . . ." or "Seeing my savings figures, I feel . . ."

We're here to help put your numbers in perspective and anchor them in reality. Once you complete the next exercise, you'll have a list of numbers to have on hand as you work your way through the rest of this book. In chapters to come, we'll refer to your debt, your income, or your existing assets—remember, you can always turn back here for easy reference.

Knowing your numbers is scary,
but it's the difference between
assuming things are good or bad
and being rooted in reality.

After all, how can we know where
to improve our finances unless we
know our money situation—both
what it is and what it should be?

KNOW YOUR NUMBERS WORKSHEET

First, get out your laptop and close all the programs. Boot up your browser and open a new tab for each of the following accounts:

- Checking account

- Savings account

- Credit report

- Retirement account

- Investing account

- Student loan account

- Credit card account

- Anything else involving money (529s, Health Savings Account, etc.)

Log into your accounts and record the numbers in the appropriate spaces on the following pages. At the end, you can step back and see all the numbers and accounts that make up your financial life.

Worried about your savings getting swept up in your usual cash flow? Try opening a separate savings account— or multiple—for different savings goals.

Bucket 1

THE BASICS

THE BASICS	
Name	
Age	
Annual income before taxes	
Additional income	
Credit score	

How to find your credit score: Many institutions—maybe even your own banking or budgeting app—let you check your credit score, also known as a FICO score, without paying a fee. Make sure you're checking through a reputable website or an institution with which you're already familiar, because some places promise free checks as a way to steal your personal information.

Bucket 2

MONEY COMING IN

YOUR CHECKING ACCOUNT
(Or checking accounts—some people have multiple accounts with different banks.)

INSTITUTION	AMOUNT	DEPOSITS
Ex. Chase checking account	$130	$1,000 paycheck from work deposited biweekly on Fridays
Total Checking:		

Bucket 3

MONEY STORED

YOUR SAVINGS ACCOUNT
(Same note applies as before! List all you have open, no matter how small the balance.)

INSTITUTION	AMOUNT	DEPOSITS
Ex. Bank of America savings account	$1,000	$50 deposits withdrawn monthly from Chase checking account
Total Savings:		

YOUR RETIREMENT ACCOUNT

INSTITUTION	AMOUNT	MY MONTHLY CONTRIBUTION (amount and percentage)	MONTHLY EMPLOYER MATCH, IF ANY (amount and percentage)
Ex. Fidelity 401k	$13,000	5%	3% match

YOUR INVESTMENTS

INSTITUTION	PRESENT-DAY VALUE	MONTHLY INVESTMENT	PORTFOLIO RISK LEVEL (if known)	DRAWS FROM
Ex. NY 529 Direct Plan	$2,000	$100	Moderate	Chase Checking

Bucket 4

MONEY OWED

YOUR DEBTS (federal student loans, private loans, personal loans, car loans, credit cards, medical bills)				
INSTITUTION	**BALANCE**	**MONTHLY PAYMENTS**	**WHEN YOU PAY**	**INTEREST RATE OR APR**
Ex. Navient	$2,400	$120	1st of the month	5%
Total Debt:				

Bucket 5

EVERYTHING ELSE

You may have some ancillary accounts, too, like one of the following (and if you don't have any of these yet, that's okay—they're specific to your individual needs and not necessarily vital to everyone):

- If your employer offers health benefits, do you have an HSA?

- Do you have any secret bank accounts?

- Do you have some sort of joint account for sharing expenses with your partner?

ANCILLARY ACCOUNTS		
INSTITUTION	AMOUNT	NOTES
Total Savings:		

START FEELING GOOD

We ask you to do this (admittedly somewhat tedious) exercise because writing out these numbers can help demystify whatever financial confusion you're feeling. The feelings you sort of batted away before—"eh, it'll all be fine" or "God, I suck at this"—can now sit quiet for a bit. Finally, you have clarity around these numbers. That's more than most people have! Whatever your numbers look like, now you can work with them.

You have these numbers, and you have us.

> **Tip:** Looking at your numbers is great and having them on hand for easy review is even better. But do not write down things like account numbers, passwords, routing numbers, or any other sensitive information.

Now is a good time to check in. How are you feeling right about now? Capture your mood in the space below. Don't get stuck in any bad feelings—simply get the feelings out of your head and onto the page.

SAVE MORE THAN
05 EVER BEFORE 05

We'll say it: saving feels good.

Watching the numbers tick up on your savings account, upping your retirement contributions, adding $10 to the cookie jar—all of it is gratifying. You can pat yourself on the back and say, "I'm an adult who plans for the future."

Because that's why we save in the first place, isn't it? To feel safe. To know that, should catastrophe strike, you'll be okay, all because **Past You was looking out for Future You.**

WHAT ARE YOU SAVING FOR?

Of course, not everyone is in the same savings situation. In the pandemic, some people were able to save more than ever before, driving the personal savings rate up to the highest level since World War II. Other people, however, found themselves struggling to handle the essential expenses of daily life.

For those who can, preparing for your uncertain future can make Present You feel more established. Even if your budget is too tight for you to save right now, it's worth doing the math to figure out when you can start saving in the future.

Before you can start saving, though, you have to first know how much your life costs and how much money you owe to other obligations. That may sound like we're trying to oversimplify the process, but think about it: setting aside money for your emergency savings fund is a great idea (and necessary—someone can always go into debt because of unforeseen circumstances). But until you know how much money you should set aside for that fund, the goal remains just that: a great idea.

Before we get started, write a list of all the reasons you want to save, whether you want to shore up your emergency savings or put money toward a vacation. For now, don't worry about what's realistic—on the following pages, we'll help you prioritize your savings goals—just get all of your savings ideas onto the page.

_____   _____

_____   _____

_____   _____

_____   _____

_____   _____

_____   _____

_____   _____

_____   _____

_____   _____

_____   _____

Tip: Saving can feel hard at times, but remember: you're doing this for you. Some savings are for the long term—like retirement—and other savings are for the short term—like your trip to Mexico. Don't feel bad about spending the savings on the things you saved for.

PREPARING FOR YOUR UNCERTAIN FUTURE

CAN MAKE
PRESENT
YOU FEEL
MORE
ESTABLISHED.

TIMING MATTERS

TAKE THE SAVINGS GOALS YOU LISTED ON PAGE 99
AND SLOT THEM INTO THESE TIME HORIZONS:

In 1 to 6 Months

SHORT TERM:

In 6 to 12 Months

MEDIUM TERM:

_____

_____

_____

_____

_____

_____

_____

In 1 to 5 Years

LONG TERM:

_____

_____

_____

_____

_____

_____

_____

YOUR SHORT-TERM GOALS

Saving for the short term can mean saving up for a one-time item—like planning a wedding or a big vacation. It could also be a very specific goal—like paying down your credit card or eliminating the last $1,000 on your student loan.

This isn't a time for jogging. This is a time for sprinting. If you need a couple hundred dollars to wipe out what's left on your credit card balance or to splurge on concert tickets, then it's time to get ruthless. A savings sprint means cutting out some unnecessary purchases for the time being (luckily, we are teaching you how to do this next!), or maybe even slashing your budget down to the bare minimum in order to sprint to the finish line (say, you want your student loan eliminated before the start of a new year).

Anyone who ran line drills in high school gym knows sprinting isn't fun. But it gets the job done, and the instant gratification you'll feel from achieving this goal will be huge.

SPRINT!

Here's an exercise to reach your short-term savings goal. You can do as many reps as you want!

Stretch

Think of this period like the setup time. Do the work you need to do ahead of time (see elsewhere in this chapter) to figure out where you can shrink your spending, cut a budget category, or otherwise find the wiggle room you need to make your savings goal. Not everyone can do this at the drop of a hat, and that's okay! Be realistic—cutting money on rent, for example, isn't going to behoove you in the long run.

Sprint

This is the hard part, but it won't last long. "Sprinting" can mean completely cutting a category of spending—takeout, if you've noticed you're spending a lot on dinner-to-go—for a given period of time.

Rest

Now take a break! Once you've accomplished your goal, you can spend freely again, but not too freely. Think of it as an unclenching from the "sprint" time. Also, if you cut all that spending on something specific, for example takeout, once you reach your short-term goal, you might consider eliminating that habit completely.

YOUR MEDIUM-TERM GOALS

These types of goals are ones you'll eventually need to tap someday. You stockpile your emergency fund, for example, because (unfortunately for everyone!) emergencies are inevitable. You add to your opportunity fund because you've set a goal of one day working for yourself.

Emergency Savings

Experts recommend stashing between three to six months of expenses in an emergency savings fund. This way, if you lose your job or run up against a medical crisis or other pitfall, you'll rest easy knowing your basic needs are handled for whatever period of time you need to recover. Because you will want this money to be easily accessible as soon as emergency strikes, we suggest keeping it in a high-yield savings account. That way, your money can grow a little, but you won't face penalties for withdrawing like you would for a certificate of deposit (CD).

Opportunity Fund

People create "opportunity funds" to buy time and freedom. Say one day you want to quit your job to start your own business or take time off. Funding this savings account can help you achieve that.

Here's a strategy to up your medium-term savings: the key to this type of savings is figuring out how much you'll need so it's not some nebulous goal.

YOUR LONG-TERM GOALS

Saving for the long term usually means saving for the biggest-ticket items in your life: things like a home purchase or retirement.

Down Payment

Buying a house is often the biggest, most momentous purchase in a person's life. Making that happen requires building up a hefty chunk of savings for a healthy down payment on a mortgage. The median national down payment is 13%, according to a 2022 report from the National Association of Realtors. Where you stash that lump sum depends on how quickly you're hoping to move. If you're still in the early stages of building up your down payment, you may want to keep it accessible, but you can also opt for something that allows your money to grow steadily over time (see Chapter 8 for more information).

Retirement

So—why do we put certain savings in investment vehicles like individual retirement accounts (IRAs) and 401(k)s? We want them to build over time, and we don't want to use these funds as an additional piggy bank for unnecessary spur-of-the-moment purchases. Stashing your retirement savings in an account like an IRA or a 401(k) allows your money to grow over the long term while taking advantage of some sweet tax benefits, not to mention the matching benefits that many companies offer their employees (aka free money!).

Here's the strategy to build your long-term savings: **automate, automate, automate.** Set those deductions from your checking account and try your damnedest to pretend the money doesn't even exist. The secret to successful long-term savings is not touching them! Make a promise to yourself: you won't draw on these reserves except in cases of dire emergency (you'll read more about this in Chapter 9).

Set 1: UP YOUR PERSONAL RATE OF SAVINGS

You'll save differently for various timelines and goals. We mapped out the major strategies on previous pages, but now is your time to put them into practice. Here's how to start:

- [ ] **Establish a reasonable savings goal.** Reasonable means you won't be missing rent, making yourself miserable, skipping out on bills, or otherwise digging yourself into a deeper hole in order to make this happen.
- [ ] **Reasonable:** I want to have $1,500 socked away over the next six months so I can take an epic end-of-summer vacay.
- [ ] **Unreasonable:** In the next month I want to pay off $30,000 on my student loans.

What's one savings goal you have and how much do you need?

_____

_____

Next, start trimming. Cut three expenses from your budget for a week. Reflect on how it felt. Many savings experts focus a bit too much on trimming the little things, like coffee or treats. Make sure you try to trim on the big stuff, too, because those savings can be multiples of those little savings. (That includes rent and what type of car to lease or where to vacation.)

Example: This week I am cutting my usual Wednesday takeout order, selecting a less expensive bottle of wine to serve at book club, and skipping Sunday brunch.

1. _____

2. _____

3. _____

Example: Cutting that Wednesday night takeout saved me $30 with delivery fees, choosing a cheaper book club wine saved me $8, and missing brunch saved me $40 (the mimosas add up, don't they??). That is a total of $78—not bad!

Saved _____ as a result. I feel _____ .

Example: I added back the brunch because my Sunday felt empty without that time with friends. But I can skip the bottomless mimosas and keep an eye on the price tag next time I go to the wine store.

Added back _____ because _____ .

Set 2: SAVE FOR
A SPECIFIC GOAL

Our fill-in-the-blank activity above walks you through some of the strategies veteran savers find key to their success: goal-setting, itemizing, and substitution among them.

Step 1: Understand Your Current Savings

How much are you currently saving each month, and how does that line up with your expectations for yourself and the goal you listed in the exercise on page 110? Ask yourself if it feels high, low, or somewhere in between.

Example: I am saving $150 a month, via automatic deduction to my high-yield savings account. It feels a bit low to me. I could do more.

Step 2: Reflect on Your Goal

Flip back to that original goal you made on page 109 (the reasonable one, not the unreasonable one). How much did you need to save for it? Write it down here again.

Example: I want to save $1,500 over the next six months so I can take an amazing end-of-summer vacation.

Step 3: Look at Those Numbers Side by Side

What is the spread between this number in Step 2 (what you need to save) and the number in Step 1 (what you're currently saving)?

Example: Oof. I want to have $1,500 saved over the next six months, but if I keep saving $150 a month, I'll only have $900 by the time I'm supposed to have met my goal.

If there's a gap between what you're saving and what you need for your goals, let's work on getting that number up. If that number still feels out of reach, then divide it by 2. And if it still feels unreachable, then you might need to reevaluate your goal altogether.

Set 3: DO IT IRL

Now examine what you learned here and take it out into the real world. That's right—the real world.

We're not going to pretend this isn't the hardest of the three exercises. We're conditioned to feel the pain of "lack" just as acutely as the joy of "more." Instead of thinking of these next steps as restrictions or cutbacks, approach them as you would cleaning out your fridge. Sure, you keep some condiments you use all the time, but those ones you don't? Don't let them crowd out the things you actually use.

Step 1: Set Aside the Essentials

Some things you simply can't trim out of the budget. You have to pay rent, for example, and you have to buy groceries. Childcare, utilities—you're not going to be touching those. So go ahead and set that money aside.

Step 2: Identify the "Unskippables"

Once you've labeled your essential expenses, move on to another category: the unskippables. This bucket includes debt payments, like student loans, car payments, credit cards, and insurance payments. If you miss a month paying these, you'll enter a spiral or take on debt that's pretty difficult to unwind.

Step 3: Find Out What Is Left Over

Once you've set aside money for the essential and unskippable expenses, look at what is left. These things are theoretically optional. Looking at all of them might feel overwhelming, so break it into chunks:

- Print out your bank and credit card statements, taking note of every line item.

- Scroll through your Venmo and Apple Pay transaction history.

- If you use expense-tracking software like Mint or YNAB, log in. Look at the numbers.

- If there's nothing left after setting aside money for the essentials and the unskippables, then you may not be ready to up your personal savings rate yet. That's okay!

Step 4: Sort

Now that you can see all the numbers right in front of you, you might feel tempted to go over every single expense. Again, think about cleaning out the fridge and clearing everything out of it to give yourself a fresh start. Before you throw something away, you read the expiration date, right? But if you do that for every single expense, you're going to want to keep them all.

In this case, we want you to take all of those "optional" expenses you found in Step 3 and put them into one big bucket.

Step 5: Hit Pause

That's right. Now it's time to go one week without any of those things you sorted out in Step 4. That means if you're paying for monthly subscriptions, don't use any of them for a week (even though you're paying for them). Have something in the cart of a store you've been browsing? Don't check it out this week. If you buy coffee every Wednesday, stop that this week as well. And if it's too overwhelming to cease all your optional expenses, just pick one type of expense to halt (such as takeout meals or online purchases).

This part of the exercise might feel the most intimidating. But hey, you can do anything for a week, right? It's just seven days! Set a calendar reminder to move on to Step 6 of this exercise after six days of temporary suspension.

HERE'S WHAT I'M GOING TO SKIP FOR THIS WEEK:

Step 6: Back to Reality

You made it! You lived!

We bet you learned a lot in the last week. We bet you felt the absence of some things and didn't even notice missing others.

Now make a list of all the things you missed, but only the ones that immediately come to mind. If you can't think of it right away, you didn't miss it much—that means it's time to cut it out of your life. Immediately automate that amount you would have spent on these items and instead send the money to a savings account, a retirement account, or education savings. You can also use this amount to pay off debt if that's the goal you want to achieve.

HERE'S WHAT I MISSED:

_____ _____

_____ _____

Voila! Instant savings boost. All it took was a handful of days and some preplanning.

Step 7: Repeat!

You heard us. Time to do those reps so you can knock out some other money goals. Go! You can repeat this exercise at any point in your life if you're looking to free up some room for savings.

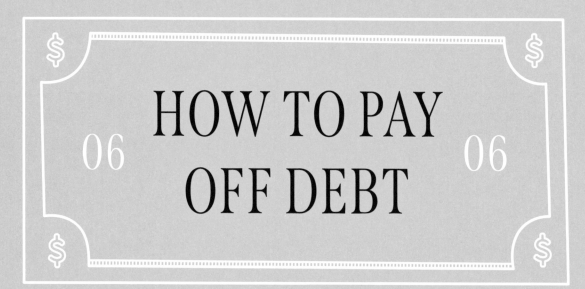

HOW TO PAY OFF DEBT

06

There are usually two schools of thought when it comes to debt: First, that all debt is bad. Second, that there's good debt and bad debt.

The first school of thought has some good roots. The idea is that living a debt-free life should be the goal, for everyone, regardless of circumstance. That's a nice idea in theory, but unfortunately, it's not very realistic in practice.

The cost of a four-year college education rose by more than 100% over the last two decades according to data from the National Center for Education Statistics. Outstanding student loan debt stands at nearly $1.6 trillion today, according to 2022 data from the Federal Reserve Bank of New York. With numbers like that, you can see why the burden of student loan debt alone severely hampers people's ability to live debt-free. On top of that, most people aren't able to purchase things like a home or a car outright. In these cases, credit is a necessary tool that helps people pay off big purchases in installments.

The second school of thought gets a little closer to how most people think about debt. Separating good debt from bad debt means putting purchases that will increase your net worth into one bucket (such as education and housing) and those that don't function as an investment into another (think the credit card debt you incurred on an Instagram shopping spree). So-called bad debts also tend to have high interest rates compared to good debt, and this includes credit cards, payday loans, and debt to pay off anything that won't be worth more later on.

So, maybe you're thinking, Alrighty, that makes sense. Good debt and bad debt. Got it.

There's just one big hiccup with that: just like anything else, too much of a good thing can become a bad thing.

In recent years, student loans have become so easy to rack up that graduates end up having an impossible amount to pay off. Similarly, housing prices in some markets have soared so high that people borrow much more than they should to buy their dream homes. Finally, some auto loans now span seven years, which sounds good in theory but will end up costing you thousands of extra dollars in interest.

In these instances, these so-called good debts mean investing in your education results in paying off student loans for decades, and borrowing more to buy your dream house can lead to foreclosure if you trip up on those high mortgage payments.

With that in mind, it may not be helpful to refer to debt as "good" and "bad" at all. Instead start thinking of your debt as "Can I afford this?"

or "Can I not afford this?" But sometimes "Can I afford this?" isn't the easiest question to answer. So here are some basic rules to help you figure that out:

- For credit card debt, being able to afford it means paying off your **full balance** every month.

- For student loans, make a plan for how you'll pay them off and whether you qualify for any loan forgiveness programs. Learn the difference between federal and private loans, and make sure you're **not late on your payments**. You can find resources on your federal loans, including a loan simulator that takes you through various options on how to finish paying your loans off in ten years, at **studentaid.gov/loan-simulator/**.

- For mortgages, make sure your monthly payments are not more than 35% of your after-tax take-home pay. Make sure you have **three to six months of mortgage payments** in your emergency fund.

- When car shopping, don't just look at the monthly payments for auto loans; look at the interest rate, too. Then consider what the monthly payments would be for a typical **three-year or five-year auto loan** and see what type of car you can afford.

- Avoid loans you can't pay back or ones with high fees. Buy-now, pay-later apps may sound like a good deal but use them responsibly— meaning you can make **all the payments on time.**

UNDERSTANDING INTEREST

Ignoring interest is like forgetting the oven is on. You think, Oh, okay, I'll turn the dial and warm up this slice of pizza and take it out, and then, before you know it, you've let too many minutes go by and your once-toasty slice of pizza is a charred hunk stuck to the bottom of your oven.

That char is the effect interest takes on your money.

Think of it like this: interest is the amount you pay to borrow money. When you repay that money, the interest is due as well. The specific interest rate will be in the fine print of your loan, and it depends on how much you're borrowing, how much you make, and how spotless your credit report is.

Low-Interest Loans: Under 10%

Federal student loans remain some of the cheapest loans around. For the past decade, interest rates have been between 2% to 9% depending on the type of loan and whether it's subsidized.

Auto loans for new cars, usually for a term of forty-eight or sixty months, have fluctuated between 4% and 7% in the past decade.

Mortgage rates change based on a number of factors. Over the last few decades, mortgage rates have stayed under 10%.

High-Interest Loans: 10% to 30%

The most common type of loans in the high-interest category is credit cards. Pay attention to the APR, the annual percentage rate, when you sign up. Many cards will offer an introductory offer where no interest is charged for the first year or first six months, but then interest rates can rocket up to nearly 30% per year. That means for every $1,000 you spend and owe, you would owe another $300 in interest over the course of a year.

Very, Very High-Interest Loans: Over 30%

Many states don't allow payday loans because of their interest rates and predatory practices. According to the CFPB, a typical two-week payday loan charges $15 per $100, which is an APR of 400%. Avoid these loans completely, or pay them off immediately if you have one.

GET OUT OF DEBT NOW

Remember playing Whac-A-Mole at the carnival? Tricky, frustrating, and difficult to win. Seriously, whose favorite carnival game is Whac-A-Mole?

Getting out of debt requires looking at all your debts at the same time, which is a very stressful activity (and why as adults we don't play Whac-A-Mole at the carnival anymore). Because of this, some people are happy to make monthly payments without making a comprehensive payment plan. We'll introduce you to an exercise that can help make sense of your debt.

Step 1

Let's first set a tone for this exercise. Think about what motivates you to pay off your debt. This is going to motivate you and keep you going.

Step 2

This is the hard part, and you may want to have a friend with you for accountability. Write down the different debts you have and include their interest rates. Start with the easy stuff that you know well: your credit card debt or your mortgage or student debt.

LOAN AMOUNT   **INTEREST RATE**

Step 3

Now let's prioritize your debt. In the space below, rewrite your debt in order—from highest interest rate to lowest. It may surprise you which loan has the highest interest.

LOAN AMOUNT   **INTEREST RATE**

_____   _____

_____   _____

_____   _____

Now that you've ordered the debt by interest rate, use this as your priority list. You'll want to pay off the debt with the highest interest rate first. Even if the highest-interest loan seems like a small amount, just get rid of it and don't think twice. In the meantime, make only minimum payments on lower-interest debt—enough to avoid incurring fees.

Step 4

Once you're done paying off the highest-interest debt, make a plan to pay off the loan with the next-highest interest. If you can, automate payments according to your goal. This will make some of the decision-making a little easier on yourself.

Step 5

Here's some extra credit: if you get bonuses or a windfall or a tax return, put that toward your debt. Already having a plan for these amounts of money helps you stay on track with your goals.

Step 6

Don't forget to celebrate each time you pay off a debt! This will help you keep motivated.

Step 7

Revisit this exercise every six months.

Step 8

Bonus! If you have time, track down small debts as well. The best way is to pull a full credit report to see if you have any unpaid debts. To order a free credit report, visit AnnualCreditReport.com. Federal law allows one free credit report a year from Equifax, Experian, and TransUnion.

Note on Bankruptcy

You may be curious about declaring bankruptcy. Filing for bankruptcy is a serious measure that involves a lot of paperwork and going to court.

A few things to know: Filing for personal bankruptcy, known as Chapter 7, will include liquidating all your assets. This can include all your bank accounts, your property, and anything you own of value.

In exchange, if your bankruptcy petition is approved, you'll be discharged from all your debts. Once you've been discharged, the creditors can't ask you for money.

Education loans, including student loans, are very difficult to discharge in bankruptcy court. There have been just a handful of cases where student loan payments were reduced in bankruptcy court.

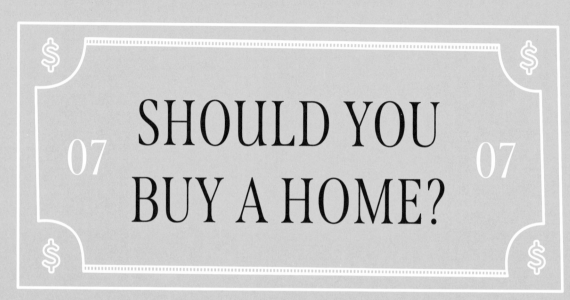

SHOULD YOU BUY A HOME?

07

07

For many families, owning a home has been the predominant method of growing wealth and ensuring financial security for decades. A little house with a white picket fence is an indelible image, one that has come to epitomize our collective understanding of the American Dream.

A lot of people feel nostalgic for those days when home ownership felt more achievable. The sad truth is that it was: over the years, young house hunters have had an increasingly difficult time finding—and buying—a starter home.

Julia's parents bought their first house as a young married couple. They got together their down payment—a little less than $10,000 or close to $22,000 in today's dollars—and found an adorable one-bedroom house with a big backyard in the South. They lived in the house when she was born and then rented it out for two years as they traveled for her father's education. Once they sold it in 1993 for a $9,000 profit, they were able to buy a bigger home in 1997 (which they still live in now). And that affordable little one-bedroom house? Today, houses in the same neighborhood sell for close to $400,000.

The supply of "entry-level" housing, which federal mortgage corporation Freddie Mac identifies as homes smaller than 1,400 square feet, is at a five-decade low. At the same time this supply was disappearing off the market, real estate costs shot up. Young house hunters say they feel frustrated, exhausted, and a host of other dejected-sounding adjectives.

But there's hope out there for motivated house hunters. More and more millennials have entered the housing market and secured their own piece of the American Dream, and real estate options like townhomes and co-ops help folks find more affordable first homes. Securing this means you're building equity and setting yourself up with an extremely helpful "forced saving" mechanism that still **pays off in the long run.**

WHY DO YOU WANT TO OWN A HOME?

Write down the reasons you want to own a home. Or if you don't, that's fine, too. Explain why:

_____

_____

_____

_____

_____

_____

_____

_____

_____

_____

_____

_____

_____

GETTING ON THE SAME PAGE

You may be buying a house with a spouse, partner, or family member. Before you start attending open houses together, however, you should have a conversation about preferences, expectations, and other hopes for your home ownership future. Below, we've included some questions to ask of your partner or family member, as well as some to answer together.

Questions to Ask Your Partner

Why is home ownership important to you? If it's not, why not?

What is negotiable and nonnegotiable for you? Examples: A thirty-minute commute? Outdoor space? A bedroom with a bathroom? A gym nearby?

How do you feel about where we live? Do you see us putting down roots here, or would you want to leave the option open for moving within the next few years?

Questions to Ask Yourselves

After we put that money toward buying a house, handling closing costs, paying for moving and more, are we still feeling okay about the money we have saved for emergencies or other financial setbacks? If yes, what new savings goals do we want to list?

How do we plan to handle homeownership-related expenses, such as money for repairs and improvements? What plan should we make now for when those costs arise?

Do we see this first house as our forever home? If not, do we see it as part of our homeownership journey? If so, which one?

A QUICK QUIZ

Let's get real. The first step to separating whether you want to own a home or you should own a home can be answered in these five questions:

1.	Would you want to buy a home on your own?	☐ YES ☐ NO
2.	Would you live in the same place for ten years?	☐ YES ☐ NO
3.	Do you have enough savings for a sizable down payment?	☐ YES ☐ NO
4.	Would you be able to fix a broken heater or broken door on your own? And if not, do you have the flexibility to hire someone for the job?	☐ YES ☐ NO
5.	Do you have a cushion in case you lose your main source of income so you don't miss any mortgage payments?	☐ YES ☐ NO

IF YOU ANSWERED NO TO ANY OF THESE FIVE QUESTIONS,
YOU'RE NOT QUITE READY!

IS HOME OWNERSHIP RIGHT FOR YOU FINANCIALLY?

How do you decide whether owning a home is right for you?

You may not want to plop down all that money if you're not planning on sticking around for the payoff or if your situation means owning a home will overstretch your budget.

Let's do the math together to figure this out. For each question below, circle the statement that best describes your situation.

What Are Housing Costs in the Area?

Use an app like Zillow or Redfin to browse available listings. Zoom out to other neighborhoods and compare prices. This will give you a sense of how much you'll need to spend. What do you make of them?

A This is what houses cost?!?!

B Okay, I played around with the mortgage calculator. It would definitely be a stretch for me financially.

C I'm pleasantly surprised! These prices seem very affordable for me.

How Much Do You Have Saved for a Down Payment and Closing Costs?

Keep in mind, this doesn't just mean "How much do I have in savings?" You'll want your down payment to still leave you with money for closing costs, emergencies, and other goals. It's also essential that you're able to make your monthly mortgage payments, plus any taxes, homeowners association (HOA) fees, or maintenance fees.

(A) I have some money saved, but I need it for my emergency fund, my opportunity fund, or another savings goal.

(B) I have been making progress on my down payment, but I'd feel more comfortable with more saved.

(C) I have saved a significant amount of money for my down payment and taken all ancillary costs into account as well.

How Stable Is Your Employment Situation?

Ask yourself: would I be able to make the mortgage if I suddenly lost my job or found myself unable to work?

(A) I don't feel stable with my job situation right now.

(B) I feel great about my employment, or I have enough savings to still make mortgage payments should I lose my job.

(C) I feel great about my employment!

Do You See Yourself Staying There Long Term?

If you could potentially move for work, don't like where you live, or have toyed with the idea of moving, then you don't want to be plunking down money on a house right now. In order to recoup closing costs and other moving expenses, conventional wisdom recommends you plan to stay somewhere for five or more years before committing to home ownership.

(A) I like it here, but it's not my forever home.

(B) I may not make a long-term life here, but I'm not going anywhere anytime soon.

(C) I'm here for the long haul!

What Is Your Credit Score?

You'll need to know this before you meet with a mortgage lender. If your credit is on the poor side, you'll likely need to work on improving it before you move on to browsing open houses. (In Chapter 4, we talked you through how to check your credit score. You can request a credit report to then cross-reference the three reporting companies as well.)

(A) After some setbacks, I am now working on improving this number.

(B) There's always room for improvement, but I'm content with my progress so far.

(C) I've worked hard to boost my numbers. I'm proud of it now!

What Is Your Debt-to-Income Ratio?

To calculate on your own: add up your monthly expenses (rent, credit card payments, debts, student loan payments, car payments, or anything else you see deducted from your balance sheet every month) and divide by your pretax income. The result is your DTI (debt-to-income), which you should configure as a percentage. You can double-check this number with a DTI calculator (often available on your bank website). Most lenders want your DTI and housing costs under 36%, although different lenders and loans have different DTI requirements.

(A) Paying down debt and improving this ratio is one of my goals.

(B) I'm getting close to my goal DTI!

(C) I'm very pleased with my debt-to-income ratio.

THE RESULTS

If you answered mostly A's: **stick to renting.**

If you answered mostly B's: **you're almost there.**

If you answered mostly C's: **you're ready to get out there.**

Based on your answers on the previous pages, you should find yourself in one of the following buckets. Read on for strategies on how to game-plan at each stage.

MOSTLY A'S: STICK TO RENTING

Here's the thing: if you can't see a future in your current city or don't know where the next couple of years may take you location-wise, it's not smart to plunk down money and buy property. By the time you close on the place, there's a chance you'll have to turn around and sell it. Without a significant amount of equity, or the money you've already invested in the house, you will likely be selling the home at a loss. Not to mention, depending on the housing market and the health of the economy, you may not be able to sell it at all.

But there's no shame in staying a renter for the time being. In the meantime, let's talk about building wealth—because there are more ways to do it than just home ownership, you know! Sections of this book are designed to help you discover compound interest, build your investing skills, and learn more about the stock market (turn ahead to Chapter 8). You can also grow wealth by paying down outstanding debt (see Chapter 6) or asking for a raise to earn more money. Maybe the prize is home ownership or maybe it's another one of the goals you outlined in an earlier chapter.

MOSTLY B'S: YOU'RE ALMOST THERE

You checked off a lot of boxes! Maybe you're confident in your stable work situation, proud of your savings, or happy to live longer in your area (maybe it's all of the above). But there's one or two outstanding items: perhaps you need to work on strengthening that credit score, or housing prices in your area are far too high right now for you to be a competitive buyer in the current market.

You won't regret waiting to buy until you're absolutely ready. The 2008 subprime mortgage crisis taught us a lot of lessons about the pitfalls of stretching yourself too far. Buying when prices are too hot, when you would have to overextend your budget to make the mortgage, when you'd be making major compromises to your "wants" list to make it work—all these things could result in serious financial calamity down the road.

We've made you a checklist on page 141. You'll find things to familiarize yourself with in the meantime so that when you're readying to hit the housing market, you'll be in awesome shape.

This is a great opportunity to play with a mortgage calculator (google it; there are a lot of options). You can see how down payments, interest rates, HOA fees, and more can affect your monthly payments.

How much do you pay in rent? And what would you pay in potential mortgage payments?

What kind of home do you want to buy? What properties are available in your area in your price range?

What neighborhood, community, or suburb do you live in now? Where would you want to move when you buy?

How much do you already have saved for a down payment? And just as importantly: Where do you plan to stash it while you wait until you're ready to buy a home?

_____

_____

_____

_____

How can you improve your credit score? Boosting that credit score even a few points can lead to big savings when you're shopping around for a mortgage. Research how you can up it by 100 or so points, even if you're already pretty happy with the one you have.

_____

_____

_____

_____

Tip: Where you put the money you've saved for a down payment is dependent on your house-hunting timeline. If you're looking to get into a home as soon as possible, then keep your down payment somewhere easily accessible, so you'll be able to tap it when the right place comes along and you need to mobilize your offer. If you're not buying for a while but want to stash the money somewhere in the meantime, consider keeping it in a high-yield savings account, and if you're waiting even longer, consider investing it in a diversified portfolio.

MOSTLY C'S: YOU'RE READY TO GET OUT THERE

Congratulations! You've taken stock of your situation and you feel ready to hit those open houses. Before you get too excited, however, let's go over some essentials.

You socked away a substantial amount of money for that down payment. Yay! But have you considered the following expenses and accounted for them in your house-hunting budget?

Things to research

- ☐ Property taxes

- ☐ Home maintenance fees (often called HOA fees)

- ☐ Closing costs, including inspection fees

- ☐ Legal fees

- ☐ The potential costs of must-do renovations or repairs

- ☐ People to talk to: realtors, mortgage lenders, and family and friends who have gone through the home-buying process

- ☐ Once you have a round figure in mind for these expenses (and leave yourself some wiggle room—depending on the housing market in your area, those prices could fluctuate), you can start looking into mortgages.

KINDS OF MORTGAGES

There are different types of mortgages, and each has its pros and cons.

- **Fixed rate:** Most commonly, you'll see the thirty-year or fifteen-year fixed-rate mortgage. The number represents the life of the loan; after making those monthly payments for thirty or fifteen years, you're estimated to have your house completely paid off. The "fixed rate" refers to the interest rate. Once it's locked in when you purchase the house, the fixed-rate mortgage classification guarantees that rate won't change (if later on, rates drop and you want to refinance, that will change—but at this stage of the game, don't worry about the word *refinance*).

- **Adjustable rate:** You'll also see adjustable-rate mortgages (aka ARMs), which differ from fixed-rate mortgages in that the interest rate can change when overall interest rates go up or down. Oftentimes people like these loans because you secure a pretty good rate on the front end. But unlike a fixed-rate mortgage, you'll have to be prepared for the rate to change, which, depending on the economic circumstances, could dramatically alter how much you pay in monthly mortgage payments.

- **Other:** There is also a wealth of different kinds of loan programs available to you depending on where you're buying, your own financial circumstances, if this is your first house or your tenth, etc. Talking through all of this with a mortgage lender can give you more insight into what makes the most sense for you, your area, and your budget.

Tip: Most importantly, know how much house can you afford. The mortgage calculator is now your best friend. Download one to your phone and play with it as you scan the listings. When you look at homes in different price points, pay close attention to the mortgage calculator breakdown.

You'll see as you tool around with the calculator that the interest rate you lock in with your mortgage servicer and the amount you already have saved as a down payment will be the two biggest factors affecting the size of your monthly mortgage payments. Keep in mind that while, historically, people have put down down payments of all sizes, more and more commonly those putting down 20% or more don't have to pay private mortgage insurance (PMI) and tend to be more competitive bidders.

You may be taken in by some of the houses you see and the loans on offer. Perhaps you look at the mortgage calculator and think, Yeah, that's a bigger payment than I expected, but it's worth it for the right house, right? Be careful. If the payment is substantially larger than what you're paying for rent now, you can easily find yourself getting "underwater" on the house or in danger of losing it altogether. When in doubt, err on the side of a more affordable mortgage payment. That's the best way to not just buy a home but also stay in one.

YOU
WON'T
REGRET
WAITING
TO BUY

A HOUSE
UNTIL
YOU'RE
ABSOLUTELY
READY.

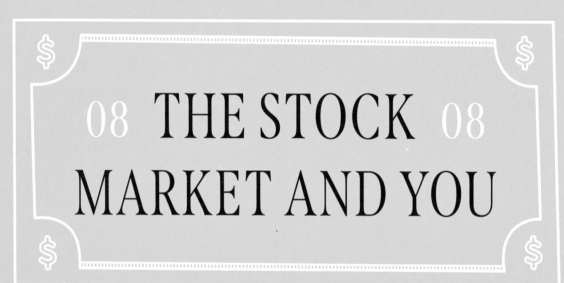

08 THE STOCK 08
MARKET AND YOU

If you don't work in finance, the stock market can seem unreal. On the news, you hear about it when it soars or plunges, but what does that mean? You may have read about certain news events giving investors confidence or jitters, but why? You hear people remark on the Dow, the S&P, meme stocks, the winners and losers—but who can explain this language, and how can they teach you?

We're here to soothe your fears. That language you say you can't understand? You don't need to be fluent to get by. The far more relevant question is this: what does the stock market have to do with you and your money?

THE BASICS

Explaining the stock market is both a constant daily activity for financial journalists and a lifetime activity for investors, researchers, and professors. We're going to skip all those deep questions of what the stock market is or isn't, the predictions of whether it'll go up or down (surprise, surprise, it does both with regularity), and the quirks and jargon surrounding it. We'll get right to the basics that are of most concern to the majority of Americans.

Here's the great thing about investing: owning stocks is a proven reliable way to build wealth in the long run. As our colleague at *The Wall Street Journal*'s "Heard on the Street" investing column put it, there's just no comparison between putting money in the bank and holding a basket of American companies' shares.

The truth is, most of us shouldn't be following the stock market on its day-to-day roller-coaster ride. The ups and downs of the market can push even those with the strongest stomachs to make bad decisions.

As far as you're concerned, you're doing long-term investing and not the kind of investing that requires you to follow the market's every move. Moving your money in and out of the market constantly isn't a good idea for the average investor. So let's talk about the steady investment accounts you should think about.

The most basic: if you have a 401(k) or IRA account, congrats! You're already an investor. The most common exposure Americans have to the stock market is through their retirement savings. When you sign up for a retirement account through your employer or on your own, you make the choice to invest that money so you'll have enough for retirement.

There are great benefits to these retirement accounts, which is why people talk about them so much. For 401(k)s, money goes in and grows tax-free. (This is not the case for a regular investment account.) Many employers offer matching contributions to help workers save for retirement.

Individual retirement accounts, referred to as IRAs, have tax benefits as well. For those starting to save for retirement early, Roth IRAs are often recommended as a way to save on taxes in retirement as money is taxed when it goes in, but grows tax-free and is not taxed when you withdraw.

Once your money goes in, you can easily buy target date funds— a leave-it-and-forget-it strategy, as it rebalances for you as you get close to retirement. You can also create your own mix of stocks and bonds, including buying mutual funds or exchange-traded funds to grow your retirement savings. Some plans now even offer cryptocurrencies as investment options as a small part of your portfolio.

BEYOND THE BASICS

(BUT STILL PRETTY BASIC!)

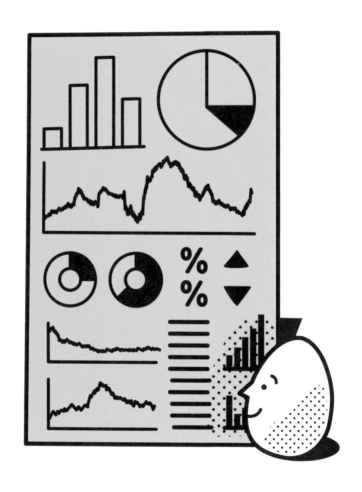

The stock market next enters our financial lives when we're looking to maximize the power of money we've already saved. Say you're starting to save some money, and while it's nice to see your savings account go up, it's not making you much more money (maybe in a high-yield savings account you earn a little more in interest—sure, that's nice, but that's not much in the grand scheme of things, considering prices will also move up over time). Once your emergency fund and short-term planned savings are taken care of, you may have some money left over that you'll save for future purposes. By the way, when we say "future," we're talking decades.

For those faraway but important goals, you want to start investing. Once you start, that pile of money you've saved up can become much bigger. It requires patience, but the chances of it paying off are good. As you get smarter about your money, you'll learn the many downsides of leaving your money sitting in the bank.

The bad news about investing is that you have to put up with the scary moments when markets dive and the thought of looking at your portfolio makes your stomach hurt. The key is not to look during those moments!

For the purposes of this book, we're mostly going to cover investing for the long term rather than short-term betting or day trading. There are a lot of other resources out there for the latter, but we wouldn't call that investing.

The basic principles of investing include learning your risk tolerance and how to invest in a way that matches how much risk you're willing to take for returns. You'll also do well to learn that there's no such thing as a sure thing in the stock market, so don't get too excited about any one stock and stick to a consistent strategy no matter what the headlines are telling you.

As you get smarter about your money, you'll learn the many downsides of leaving your money sitting in the bank.

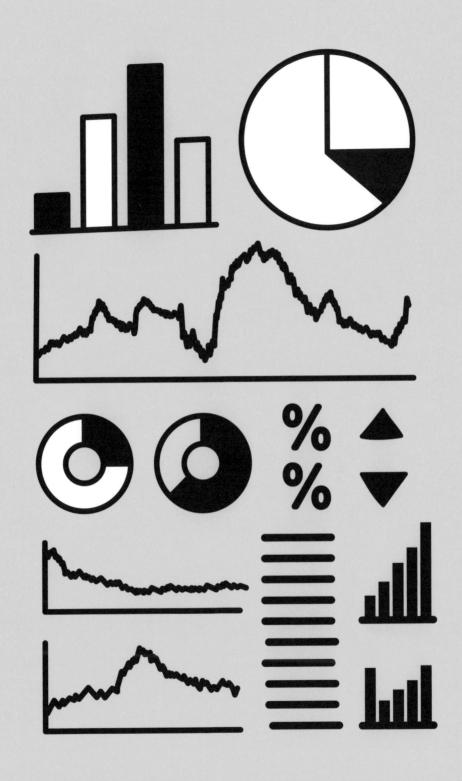

Stick out the bad days with the good. Time in the market is the most important factor in investing, not timing the market.

HOW TO START INVESTING

 To learn about all these principles, use this QR code to take our WSJ Investing Challenge, which will take you through five activities and show you investing basics. If you're looking for more of an immediate start to investing, we'll take you through beginner ways to invest and the things you need to know, followed by a script on how to talk to a financial adviser.

If you're getting into investing with the aim to make a quick buck, or your only question about investing is "What stock should I buy?" we need to take a few steps back.

The first thing to know is that buying just one stock, or a few stocks that are similar, isn't a good investment strategy. A core tenet of investing is diversification, meaning having different types of equities to reduce risk. If your idea of investing is buying $100 of stock in your favorite company, or in a stock your friend says will for sure double your money in a week, we're here to tell you that's not investing.

Another thing to know is that investing is not the kind of thing you do for a week here and there. Though discount brokerages mean that trading stocks is free (or close to free) these days, if you're not willing to spend time in the market—and its ups and downs—you're not ready to invest.

CHECKLIST

On that note, let's make sure you're financially ready to start investing. If you're not, don't worry—you'll find out what you need to work on so you can start.

Use this checklist to see if you're ready to start investing in an account separate from your retirement funds:

☐ You already have enough money to handle your monthly expenses, including housing, debt payments (student loans, car payments, credit cards), basic costs (food and other necessities), and monthly bills (utilities, cellphone plan, insurance plans, gym, etc.).

☐ You have paid off all your high-interest debt.

☐ You have an emergency fund equivalent to six months of expenses.

☐ You have a separate savings account from your emergency fund, specifically for things you're saving for in the next couple of years, including vacations, a new winter jacket, a big party (such as a wedding), or even a down payment for big purchases such as a car or a home. If you're unsure about how much to keep in this separate account, $5,000 to $10,000 is a good start.

☐ You're contributing to your retirement account to take full advantage of any matching benefits.

☐ You're ready to start thinking long term about things, not just for your money but for yourself. You get the feeling you'll feel a lot better knowing you have a retirement fund started or that you have some savings stashed away for your kids' college education.

I AM INVESTING FOR:

1. Myself

2. My future

3. My kids' education

4. This other reason

Next, circle what you're investing for before you open a brokerage account.

Tip: Another reason not to get too excited about just one stock: it's really hard to make money by stock-picking, which is why you want to fill your basket with many types of eggs.

IF YOU CIRCLED 1 . . .

Start by opening a brokerage account.

Investing for yourself is great! First, open a brokerage account to start putting your money to work. There are plenty of online brokers these days, from Fidelity to Robinhood, that offer trading for free with no account minimum.

Next, start a portfolio and decide what you want to put money into. Nearly all experts will tell you no good will come from stock-picking on your own. Not only does this require a lot of studying (including learning how to research stocks and funds and how to diversify your investments), but it is against the odds that you'll make more money, because so many companies don't end up performing as well as funds with lots of companies in them.

What to Invest In

That's why there are thousands of investment products designed to help regular investors, but of course the fine print here is to make sure you look at the fees. Funds come with fees, called expense ratios—this is the cost you pay annually for your investment to be managed. Expense ratios are percentages of your total investment that you owe every year to your fund manager. For example, an expense ratio of 0.78% means you'll pay $78 for every $10,000 you invest.

That may not sound like much, but these fees can really eat into your returns. Say you are investing $50,000 with a 6% annual rate of return. The difference between a 0.2% expense ratio and a 1% expense ratio could mean having a $270,000 nest egg thirty years from now, compared with around $212,000. Your nest egg is some $58,000 smaller because of that seemingly small 1% fee.

That's why it's important to research the funds you're putting your money into. Whether an expense ratio is high or low really depends on the type of investment. The more DIY an investment is, the lower the fee should be. The more hand-holding it provides, the higher the fees.

In recent years, low-cost index funds have become extremely popular since some carry extremely low fees, at less than 0.05%. A general rule of thumb is to look for fees less than 0.10% a year.

Instead of stock-picking, investing in low-cost mutual funds or exchange-traded funds (ETFs) means paying a small fee to have your money diversified for you. Another easy way to start investing is to put your money on America's biggest companies by buying into an index fund, which holds all the stock of a particular index. Popular index funds include ones that track the S&P 500 (meaning you're investing in the five hundred largest American companies) or the entire U.S. stock market (such as Vanguard's popular Total Stock Market Index fund).

You can also pay for a robo-adviser, algorithms that will help you balance your portfolio and rebalance based on what your investment goals are. Using robos is less DIY than buying funds yourself, so they tend to cost more. Fees range up to 0.9%.

Both of these options tend to cost less than working with a human financial adviser, which can cost 1 to 2%, so always think about what you feel comfortable with in terms of fees, risk, and how much you want to DIY versus pay for someone to help you.

Write down some investments you're interested in researching.
Use the space below to write down some investments you've heard
of or are interested in investing in and what the fee/expense ratio is.

_____

_____

_____

_____

_____

IF YOU CIRCLED 2 . . .

Find investment accounts with benefits.

Take a good look at your retirement accounts and consider other
types of investments, such as individual retirement accounts or a
health savings account.

Thankfully, saving for retirement includes a lot of tax benefits. We've
gone over the 401(k) in Chapter 1, and remember, you can look in
your plan to decide how you'll invest the money you're contributing.
But to up your game with your retirement savings, look into IRAs,
including Roths. The different tax benefits of these accounts mean
you can strategize which mix of accounts would give you the best
returns based on your current income and your expected income in
retirement. IRAs provide more flexibility than some 401(k)s.

With all those tax benefits comes a pretty big caveat: because these
accounts are designed for long-term investing, you can't withdraw

money from them without penalty until you're 59½, with some exceptions. This age is set by the government, and by 73, you are required to start drawing down these accounts. There are also limits on how much you can contribute each year.

Another way to save for retirement is to open a Health Savings Account if it's offered by your company. Health care is one of the highest bills retirees have to pay, so having an investment account for these future expenses is a good idea.

HSAs are unique in the triple tax advantage they offer: if you opt for a high-deductible health plan, you can contribute to an HSA by setting aside pretax earnings without paying federal or state income tax, unless you live in California or New Jersey. From there, that money can be invested and grow tax-free. Additionally, if you have kept receipts showing it was used for medical expenses, this money can be withdrawn tax-free before retirement, which can't be done with a 401(k) or an IRA.

IF YOU CIRCLED 3 . . .

Open a 529 savings account.

The main attraction of a 529 account is the sweet tax savings you get while saving for your child's education. Most states offer tax benefits for the money you put in, and, importantly, the money grows tax-free in funds determined by your state's saving plan. You can withdraw the money tax-free as long as you use it for education expenses, including tuition, books, room and board, and even student loans. Unused amounts can be given to another family member, including your grandchildren.

The best time to open an account is when your child is born or adopted. Automate an amount to deduct automatically from your bank account and watch the money grow over time.

IF YOU CIRCLED 4 . . .

Let's consider the reason you're investing so you can think of an appropriate strategy.

If your goal is to make profit in the short term, know that there's a lot of risk involved and decide how much you're going to invest accordingly. Investing should be a long-term, some say lifelong, activity and fails too often as a way to make fast money.

For example, if you're investing in order to take a vacation, just be prepared that you may not hit the amount you'll need for that vacation for a number of years. Maybe a decade depending on what you invest in and the economic conditions. Safe investments generally grow slowly, and investments that promise big returns come with big risks. All returns, except for the ones in tax-advantaged accounts for retirement or education, have tax consequences or penalties.

This is especially important to remember if you're investing for fun. Some people want to buy a share in their favorite company or a stock everyone is talking about. In this case, these are gambles and not investments, and you should be prepared to lose every penny you put down. If you can't afford, or stomach, that sort of loss, don't play assuming you'll break even.

A SCRIPT FOR TALKING TO
A FINANCIAL ADVISER

Some of you may be looking for more beyond the DIY-style guidance we've outlined (and, of course, elsewhere in this book). Researching a financial adviser may be a good idea if you've made it this far into this book and have bigger, more specific questions about your money plans and your hopes for your financial future.

Sarah Behr, founder of Simplify Financial Planning in San Francisco, recommends turning to the National Association of Personal Financial Advisors and the XY Planning Network, two great resources that allow you to search for local advisers by specialty and fee structure.

While it's easier to go with someone that your friend or family recommends, it's important to do your research for personal referrals. Look at their certification and fee structure to make sure you're aware—and revisit goals (maybe some of the ones you first listed in the opening pages of this book!) you'll want to discuss with them. Make sure they are a fee-only planner, someone who takes a flat fee for their services rather than receiving a commission. This is a person who will act as a fiduciary and put your financial interests first.

Once you've made your list of potential people to contact, you'll want to gather some basic materials to share: tax forms, retirement accounts, and other financial documents pertaining to the goal you want to discuss. Then, the big part—send the initial email. Below, we have a script for how you can first open the door to finding the financial adviser that best fits you and your goals.

Hello, **[Adviser Name Here],**

I am a **[insert your age, profession, and location here],** reaching out because I am looking for a financial adviser who can work with me to **[state one or two goals here, such as growing your financial understanding, managing debt, or preparing for a big money milestone]** . . .

I received your contact information from **[Explain how you found them! Did you research advisers in your area? Search through a database or article of recommendations? Did you get a referral from a colleague or friend?]** . . . Reading through your website, I was attracted to **[list some of the things that prompted you to reach out, such as an appealing fee structure or expertise in your particular industry]** . . . I was hoping to set up an introductory meeting to talk more about your fee structure and the frequency of our meetings.

Looking forward to hearing back from you,

[Your Name Here]

Use this page for taking notes during your calls with financial advisers.

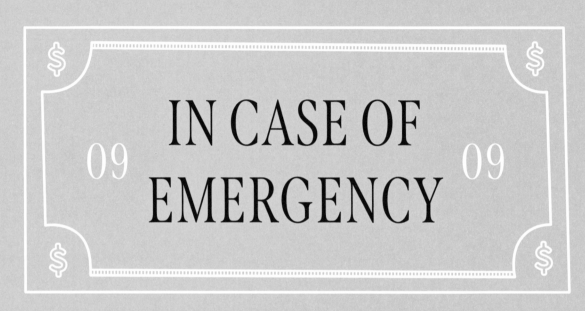

IN CASE OF EMERGENCY

09

Emergencies are going to happen, as much as we don't want them to. We all lived through 2020 and saw this firsthand. We witnessed even the most researched, actionable, well-intentioned plans thwarted by an unforeseen global health crisis.

In your financial life, there are innumerable crises that can pop up out of nowhere to jettison your goals: job loss, medical debt, Mother Nature. The key to a strong financial plan is keeping the unplanned at the very forefront of your mind, as odd as that sounds.

This chapter is designed to help you do just that: plan around the things that seem impossible to plan for. We promise it's more doable than it seems.

FACE YOUR FEARS

Everyone has fears, financial or otherwise. The thing about fears is, it's so much better to know them. Many people would say that's the first step to feeling okay.

List your financial fears here:

_____   _____

_____   _____

_____   _____

_____

List five things you can do over the next year that will help combat your financial fears:

1. _____

2. _____

3. _____

4. _____

5. _____

"The best plans have to acknowledge a complete inability to know what will happen in the future," said Meg Bartelt, financial adviser with Flow Financial Planning in Bellingham, Washington. "It could be inflation, a stock market crash, a pandemic that shuts down the world—you plan for those things without knowing the specifics, just by building in a large room for error. If your plan only works when things happen exactly within a very narrow band of possibilities, then that plan is pretty fragile."

So, how do you teach yourself to expect the unexpected?

First, you accept the inevitability of an emergency. It happens to everyone, and it's likely not your fault. Once you understand you can't live a life void of it, you won't be as shocked and troubled when catastrophe arrives at your door. Next, you have contingency plans in place so that when the horrible arrives—your car breaks down, your surgery isn't covered by insurance, or your tax bill calculations were way off—you can break the glass and pull the emergency lever.

What are some financial emergencies you've encountered in the past?

How did you solve them?

Have contingency plans in place so that when the horrible arrives you can break the glass and pull the emergency lever.

When faced with a financial emergency, remember these things:

This Is Why You Have Savings

Remember the emergency fund we discussed building in Chapter 5? Well, times like these are exactly why we've been building it. No one likes seeing money leave their account, but in this case, that is the sole purpose of stocking this fund to begin with.

Car trouble, urgent care visits, home repairs—sometimes life happens, and you have to hit the pause button on your savings goals.

This Is Why You Have Insurance

At the moment, you may cringe at the idea of an extra expense, but in the future, you'll be so grateful that Past You moved on from the cringe and hit "buy" on the policy that's saving your butt and your wallet.

Health Insurance

Ah, the big one. You're likely already very familiar with health insurance, as it's the kind of policy that comes up most often in daily conversation with parents, friends, or coworkers. Health insurance helps you handle big health expenses and medical debt.

In the United States, you can stay on your parents' insurance policy until you turn twenty-six. After that, you're responsible for securing coverage on your own. If you work a full-time job with benefits, pay very close attention to open enrollment season. That's when you can choose your health insurance coverage or make changes to your previous elections. You'll want to read all the fine print here.

If you're unable to take advantage of employer-sponsored health insurance, you can seek out private health insurance, state exchanges, group or trade association health insurance, or, depending on your income bracket, Medicare. Remember: any policy is better than being uninsured. Should an accident or illness befall you, you could find yourself mired in tens of thousands of dollars of debt incurred from your medical care.

Tip: If you have employer-sponsored coverage but are unsure about which health insurance plan to choose, set up a meeting with your human resources department or ask a colleague how they decided upon which plan was right for them.

Disability Insurance

Disability insurance is different from health insurance in that it protects you should you find yourself suddenly unable to work for an indeterminate length of time. The prospect of losing out on your salary, benefits, and other perks of work is scary, but while health insurance should help cover your health expenses, disability insurance could help provide for the other costs that accrue in daily life. Many employers offer disability insurance—both long-term and short-term—as part of their benefits packages for employees. Check with your human resources department first to see if this is on offer, or research how much it would cost you to purchase it on your own.

Life Insurance

This is important, especially if you are taking care of other people financially. Should the worst happen, you want to know your parents, kids, or partner will be able to pay the bills. Start looking into insurance options now. The most basic and easy type of life insurance is the twenty-year or thirty-year term life insurance, which you can convert to a permanent policy later on. Getting this policy started when you're younger and healthier means lower monthly premiums for the long term. A quick medical exam is usually required, but it's worth comparison-shopping to see which firms can offer you the best rate.

Other Insurance

Depending on your individual circumstances, you may require other policies, such as dental, vision, or auto insurance. There's even pet insurance these days. If you're a homeowner, look into homeowner's and flood insurance. Renters insurance is also worth considering if you're worried about theft or damage.

> **Tip:** Now, reading all those insurance options in a row may have spooked you a bit. But just because we listed them all doesn't mean you *need* them all. Read the fine print and think carefully about what protection you need and how much you can afford.

ORDER OF OPERATIONS

How do you handle a financial emergency? What funds do you draw from first, what spending do you cut back on, and how do you take on debt in the least destructive way to your financial life?

Here's what order to use as you scale back your finances, in case of emergency.

1. Try Negotiating

You'd be surprised what can be negotiated and with whom you can negotiate. Your landlord, your credit card company, your student loan servicer—when you're facing desperate times, trying everyone is worth a shot. Here's a list of people to keep in mind to ask what options there are and whether you can work something out:

- Landlord
- Credit card company
- Customer service representative for a service you use
- Hospital billing
- Debt collector

2. Stop Saving

Maybe you have scheduled automatic deductions or you save with a "change-rounding" app. Ceasing your savings progress may feel scary, but when you need to do it, you need to do it. Don't think too hard about the savings gains you're worried about forgoing; for now, focus on putting that money to use. Rest assured you'll be able to catch up one day. In the meantime, make sure you heed the following:

- **Do this in stages.** You don't need to completely turn off all savings mechanisms while you're handling a crisis. You can stop saving gradually, first by reducing your usual amount of monthly savings, and then by lowering your retirement contributions—or a combination of both. Doing this in stages can help shore up what you have left over and (most crucially, experts say) won't leave you mired in feelings of failure or self-disappointment.

- **Don't feel bad.** Beating yourself up about stopping saving won't help you weather whatever storm necessitated this move in the first place. If you're struggling with feelings of guilt or shame, read on to Step 3.

- **Schedule a restart date.** This keeps you accountable to your savings goals, but when the bad stuff passes, this "start saving again" date on the calendar will also prevent your regular, everyday spending from swallowing up the extra room you built into your budget when times were tough.

3. Deplete Your Emergency Fund

This is why you have an emergency fund, remember? Don't beat yourself up for tapping that account when catastrophe strikes. But in order to safeguard your emergency plan for the future, remember the following:

- **Make a plan to build it back up.** You may be thinking, It took me years to save x amount! And wow, maybe it did! When you're back on your feet, you'll build this back up. Set a timeline.

- **Extend your time horizon.** You may have been building up the fund with a goal in mind and find it hard to draw down the account. But this is why you have the account in the first place—it's a lifeline for true emergencies. Make a long-term plan to build this back up.

> **Tip:** Rebuilding your emergency savings can feel like a herculean task, but remind yourself: you already did this before! Set a date on the calendar for when you'll have your income stream restored, when a new paycheck will hit your bank, etc. This is the date when you can start automating deposits into your emergency savings accounts.

4. Take On Debt (in the Most Responsible Way Possible!)

Look, we'd love to pretend that in an ideal world, you can check off the top three steps here and avoid running up your credit card balance, taking out a loan, or opening a new card. But realistically, sometimes those are your only options. There are ground rules to consider, however.

- **Talk to someone.** You may not have a personal financial adviser, but many organizations offer resources and consultations for free to those in need. Before you decide what amount and kind of debt to take on, talk to someone at one of these groups, such as the National Association of Personal Financial Advisors or the Association for Financial Counseling & Planning Education.

- **Consider the interest rate.** There are loans with high interest and loans with low interest. Asking a friend or family member for a personal loan could even mean zero interest, depending on the relationship. If you're opening a new card or putting money on an existing one, look at the annual percentage rate, or APR (more on this in Chapter 6).

- **Watch out for scams or traps.** Getting a loan should not be easy. Be ultra-wary of anyone offering you a seemingly hassle-free way out of a bad situation. Cash-advance spots and payday lenders make getting the money seem easy but then turn around and charge interest rates as high as 30% and all the way up to 400%. Don't fall for it.

5. Tap into Some Other Lines of Credit or Relief

When the debts mount or the payments fall behind or go delinquent, people look for money in other places. Homeowners have several options here: they can look into home equity lines of credit or cash-out refinancing. Those with retirement savings can make withdrawals from 401(k) or individual retirement accounts, which should be a last-ditch option.

Many of these options come with a hefty tax penalty and talking with a financial adviser or a relief organization (see above for low-cost or free options) can help you weigh the pros and cons of such measures.

What is your emergency plan? Capture it below.

_____

_____

_____

_____

_____

Don't let making this plan discourage you! Even the most diligent of savers encounter times when they temporarily stop saving or dip into the fund for some emergency money. Remember: this is why you built up this savings in the first place.

FINANCIAL SELF-CARE

10
10

We believe financial self-care days should also be cozy days. That means wearing the fluffiest cardigans, queuing up soothing lo-fi beats, and brewing fancy beverages.

When we set aside time like this to get our lives in order, we like to move in two modes: gathering (like pulling up all account info so you have all the information right in front of you) and hunting (tracking down the fees you want to eliminate or canceling recurring charges you decide are no longer worth the money).

We like to emphasize the coziness because we associate that warm, snuggly feeling with self-care. Sure, looking at a bank statement isn't the same as unwrapping a lavender face mask, but both give that "I just did something good for myself" high we're always chasing.

BOURREE'S FINANCIAL SELF-CARE DAY SCHEDULE

8 a.m.: Wake Up and Stretch

My self-care day will involve a lot of sitting down, so I start the day with stretching or a little bit of yoga or a run in the park to get my blood flowing.

9 a.m.: Coffee, Cereal, and Computer

I listen to music and start by logging into all of my financial accounts and taking a big-picture look at how I'm doing, from checking and savings accounts to retirement and health expenses accounts.

10:30 a.m.: Goal Progress

Based on my review of my accounts, I give myself one or two priorities for the rest of the day. Do I want to work on my budget or long-term savings? Make a plan to up my credit score or figure out a few things for my taxes?

11 a.m.: Break

I take a walk to gather materials for lunch, either a salad or a sandwich. Working on my finances makes me not want to spend money on takeout.

12 p.m.: Lunch + Let My Mind Wander

While I prep and eat lunch, I let my mind wander to think about what I'd love to achieve and less about how to get there. This helps motivate me.

1 p.m.: Today's Main Goal

I will accomplish one big task today. I only pick one. Here's a list of recent big tasks I've worked on:

1. Rebalancing my retirement accounts.
2. Check in and set (or reset) all my automated payments and savings to meet goals.
3. Pull a free credit report on myself to check that it's correct, then make a plan to keep my credit score above 750.
4. Apply for a mortgage to see what rate I'd get.
5. Make a budget for a life event, whether it's an upcoming vacation or holiday season.
6. Check on my life and rental insurance policies.
7. Run the numbers. Can I pay off more debt each month?
8. Identify things I purchased that I don't need (and return the items if that's still an option!).

4 p.m.: Subscriptions

I end my self-care day by checking on recurring payments. I always cancel a few things (and never end up missing them!).

I let my mind wander to think about what I'd love to achieve and less about how to get there.

JULIA'S FINANCIAL SELF-CARE DAY SCHEDULE

10 a.m.: Break Out the Milk Frother

Playing at-home barista always puts me in a good mood.

11 a.m.: Know Your Numbers

You remember this exercise from Chapter 4! I know it may have felt like a lot of work in the moment, but personally, I like to repeat this on a regular basis. I think of it as a financial wellness check-in: How are my savings looking? What's the credit card balance? Where are my investments? Once I have all my numbers in front of me, I can gauge how well I'm doing regarding progress toward certain goals.

12 p.m.: Strikethrough Time

Once I've pulled my numbers and taken stock of my progress, I like to review my latest bank statement and circle any charges that don't make immediate sense to me. This is the best way to spot sneaky fees, lapsed subscriptions, and anything else that makes me go, "I was paying for that? Really?"

1 p.m.: Lunch Break

I don't know about you, but saving money makes me hungry. And after the last activity, you saved a good chunk of it! That means it's time to toast (with, in my case, pan con tomate).

2 p.m.: Adjust Deductions

I believe in the power of automated deductions. I owe all my greatest savings goals to the power of "set it and forget it." So on a self-care day, I like to go check in on those deductions. Have I felt the sting of inflated prices lately? Then maybe I should reduce my deductions by a dollar or two. Or, conversely, did I recently get a raise or a bonus? Then let's increase those deductions by just a bit. The more I can save without knowing, the happier I am.

3 p.m.: Shut the Laptop and Do a Face Mask

I search spa music on Spotify, grab a fresh-scented sheet mask, and close my eyes. My face has done a lot of work in front of the computer today! Now it is time to bask in the glow of a job well done.

YOUR FINANCIAL SELF-CARE DAY SCHEDULE

8 a.m.

9 a.m.

10 a.m.

11 a.m.

12 p.m.

1 p.m.

2 p.m.

3 p.m.

4 p.m.

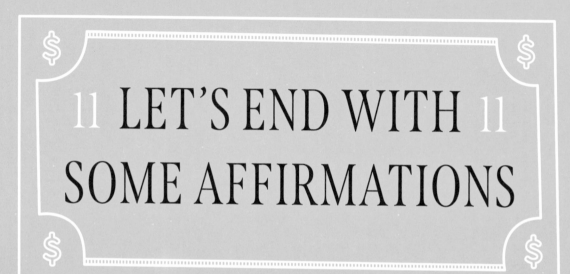

11 LET'S END WITH 11
SOME AFFIRMATIONS

Affirmations are positive phrases you repeat to yourself. People speak them out loud, write them down in a notebook, or simply recite them quietly to themselves. Research shows that with repetition, self-affirmation can help increase feelings of self-worth and confidence, even rewiring our neural pathways to expand our understanding of ourselves and our self-competence.[1]

> **Tip:** A single self-care day schedule is helpful, but thinking about your financial journey on a frequent—and positive!— basis can help neutralize negative feelings about your money capabilities you've internalized over the years.

1. The research was published in the April 2016 issue of *Social Cognitive and Affective Neuroscience*.

HOW DO THEY WORK?

In essence, affirmations protect you from yourself. They may feel corny, but these positive phrases can help curb negative thinking or undo self-deprecating narratives you tell yourself about your life and your attitudes.

Typically, people rely on affirmations almost like little doses of medicine. You need to pop a Tums when heartburn keeps you up at night; similarly, you need to lean on one of these affirmations below next time you feel your mind spiraling to a place of negative self-talk.

I'm not the only one with these feelings.

Use if: you have bad feelings about your money situation.

I have the money I need for now.

Use if: you're always saying "I'm broke" or stressing out at the balance in your bank account. Are you making your rent on time? Stocking your fridge with food? Not falling behind on big bills or looming debt payments? That is a success in and of itself. Sometimes we spend too much time focusing on the things we can't afford rather than the things we are already affording. That is worthy of celebration.

I make good money decisions.

Use if: you think of yourself as "inexperienced" or often refer to yourself as someone "bad with money." Have you taken the steps to learn more about personal finance? Have you thought hard about applying those steps to your own life? That is a win! Keep in mind that second-guessing your decision-making is a recipe for disaster. Once you start doubting your own ability, you'll never have confidence in your choices. And you've already made some great ones, like picking up this book and arriving at this page.

I have a plan for that.

Use if: anxiety about "What could happen???" is eating away at any sense of security you manage and to which you cling. Is any plan truly foolproof? For that matter (given what you've read in the previous chapters), is any plan 100% recession- or pandemic-proof?

I survived [insert biggest financial blunder]. I can survive this.

Use if: you're still feeling the sting of past financial woes. You feel you're struggling now. Remember back to the last time you struggled. Did you make it to the other side? And look at where you are now.

I don't have to spend like that.

Use if: you're trying to change your spending habits. Maybe every time you look at your bank account you think, I didn't even want that. You need to hold on to that feeling in order to curb your spending.

There's no hurry.

Use if: you compare your timeline to that of your friends and peers. There is no "right time" to buy a house. There is no "right" level of life for you to unlock at a given time. You have the time! Your goals can happen when they happen.

I have what I need.

Use if: you find yourself thinking, There are so many things I can't afford. Do you find yourself laundry-listing the numerous things you want to buy but feel you can't? Put those thoughts aside; you may have everything you already need.

I can do a little thing and it will count.

Use if: you feel overwhelmed by your various goals, problems, or fears. There's always one thing you can tackle.

<u>I can ask (or pay) for help.</u>

Use if: you know you need a friend, family member, or a professional to help with a given task. You're not an accountant, after all! This is why people hire accountants! (Hi, accountants—thank you for what you do. Especially around tax season.)

> **Tip:** Feel free to mix and match these affirmations should your circumstances or goals change.

ADD YOUR OWN
AFFIRMATIONS HERE

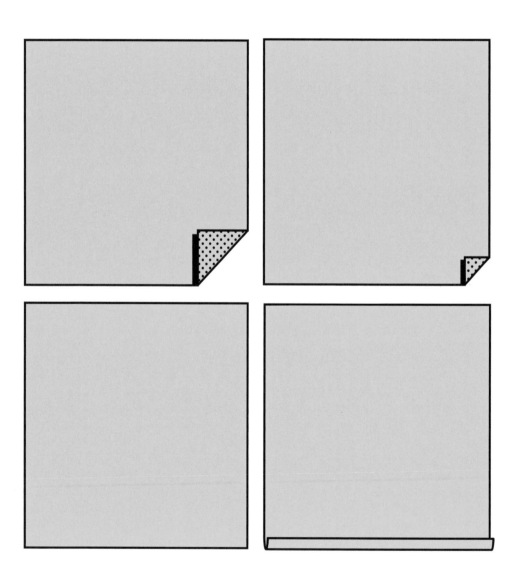

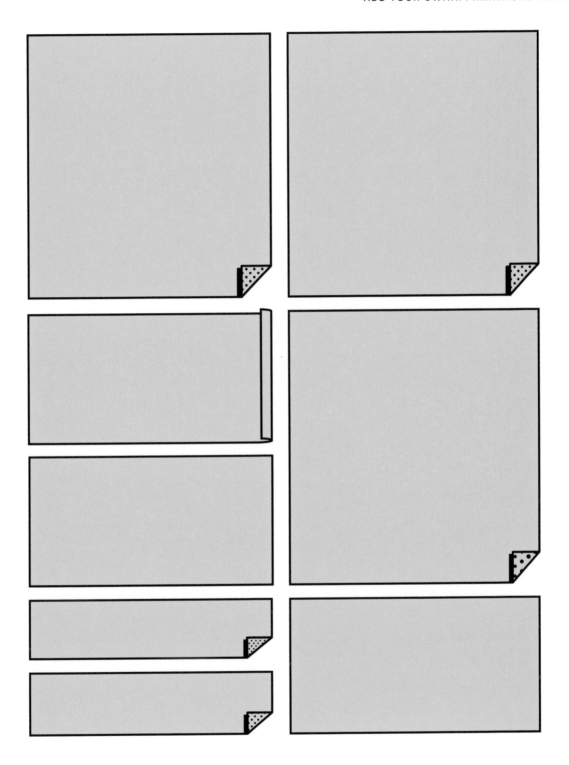

YOU'VE JUST FINISHED *THE NEWRULES OF MONEY*– OUR NEW RULES OF MONEY.

WHAT ARE *YOUR* NEW RULES OF MONEY? WRITE THEM HERE.

_____

_____

_____

_____

_____

_____

_____

_____

_____

_____

_____

_____

_____

_____

_____

_____

#WSJNEWRULES

TELL US YOUR MONEY RULES

HOW TO PUT THEM INTO PRACTICE

Now you have affirmations you can turn to when you need an extra confidence boost. Here are some ideas on how to put them into practice:

- Share an affirmation with a friend and make a pact that the next time one of you needs to hear it, you'll text the other one.

- Copy the affirmation out on a Post-it and stick it to your bathroom mirror. As you chip away at a mountain of debt or head into your big salary negotiation meeting, take the time to look into the mirror and absorb this affirmation. You have a plan. You are taking steps toward it. Now—onward!

- Put the words of a given affirmation to music. Hum them to yourself when you need the reminder.

- Type the chosen affirmation out in a phone alarm or recurring calendar reminder. When the phrase pops up on your screen, take a deep breath and repeat the words to yourself.

Last word: On the next page we shout out all the people who helped us make this book. But first, we wanted to thank YOU— thank you for reading this book, for doing the exercises, and going on this journey with us.

Now go thank someone else who helped make your money journey more fun.

Acknowledgments

Our biggest bouquet of thanks to our literary support crew and the fabulous designers, editors, production managers, and staff at Clarkson Potter and Penguin Random House, in particular Lise Sukhu, Joyce Wong, Luisa Francavilla, and Danielle Deschenes. Our editor, Angelin Adams, was a rock for us, holding our hands through the book process and helping us think creatively for years to bring this workbook to completion. Special thanks to our agent, Marya Spence, at Janklow & Nesbit for championing this project in its earliest days and helping us envision its future. And to Gabbie Van Tassel, whose passion for personal finance led her to reach out initially and get this workbook off the ground.

Our generous colleagues at *The Wall Street Journal* who answered our questions, shared their expertise, and cheered us on along the way. This book wouldn't have been half as fun without our fabulous colleagues and editors: the personal finance team which has been our home the last few years; Nikki Waller and Jeremy Olshan for their thoughtful edits and unfailing support; Mike Miller for shepherding it from the start to the finish line; Charles Forelle for always believing in our crazy ideas. Huge thanks also to Serena Solin for checking our facts and working with multiple long email threads.

We're grateful to work in a newsroom that values collaboration and peer support. We, of course, have to make special mention of the ingenious teams we worked with to launch the Nest Egg Game and the WSJ Six-Week Money Challenge. Those two projects inspire us endlessly to create and continue to drive us forward in experimentation.

Readers no doubt smiled flipping through the illustrations in this book. That's all thanks to Jess Kuronen, our collaborator for all things illustrations. Thank you for bringing your stellar eye and incomparable talent to these pages.

We will always be thankful to our sources—the financial advisers, scholars, and real people who shared their money stories with us—for trusting us. Without you, there's only guessing in the dark about the real universal financial concerns we all share and see. With you, we can navigate this space together.

A note from Julia: I'd like to thank my big, loud, funny family—I just know they are going to move this book from the back shelves to the front shelves of any bookstore they ever enter for the rest of my life. I'd also like to thank my wonderful community of friends. Even when I felt overwhelmed by the sheer size of this work, you encouraged me to remember the reader and, cheesy as it sounds, write from the heart. Speaking of heart, my biggest thanks goes to Rachel, who took on extra dog walks, cooked up big bowls of tomato soup, and sat up in bed in the middle of the night with me so I could talk out the finer points of this book. Your patience and care made this book possible.

And one from Bourree: This book is dedicated to my late mother, the first person to teach me about money. I owe many thanks to my father, family, and friends who encouraged me to write despite setbacks, supported me in moments of doubt, and believed in me. My colleagues, former and current, who love personal finance—it challenged and encouraged me to charge forward on the topic. My dedicated husband, David, gave me the priceless gift of time by watching our son on a dozen Sundays so I could write in a toddler-free environment. I didn't expect we'd have a child before I wrote a book, so I'm extra thankful for a partner who likes saving money (and spending it) as much as I do.

NOTES

All rights reserved.
Published in the United States by Clarkson Potter/Publishers, an imprint
of Random House, a division of the Crown Publishing Group, New York.
ClarksonPotter.com

CLARKSON POTTER is a trademark and POTTER with colophon
is a registered trademark of Penguin Random House LLC.

ISBN 978-0-593-23423-5

Printed in China

10 9 8 7 6 5 4 3 2 1

First Edition